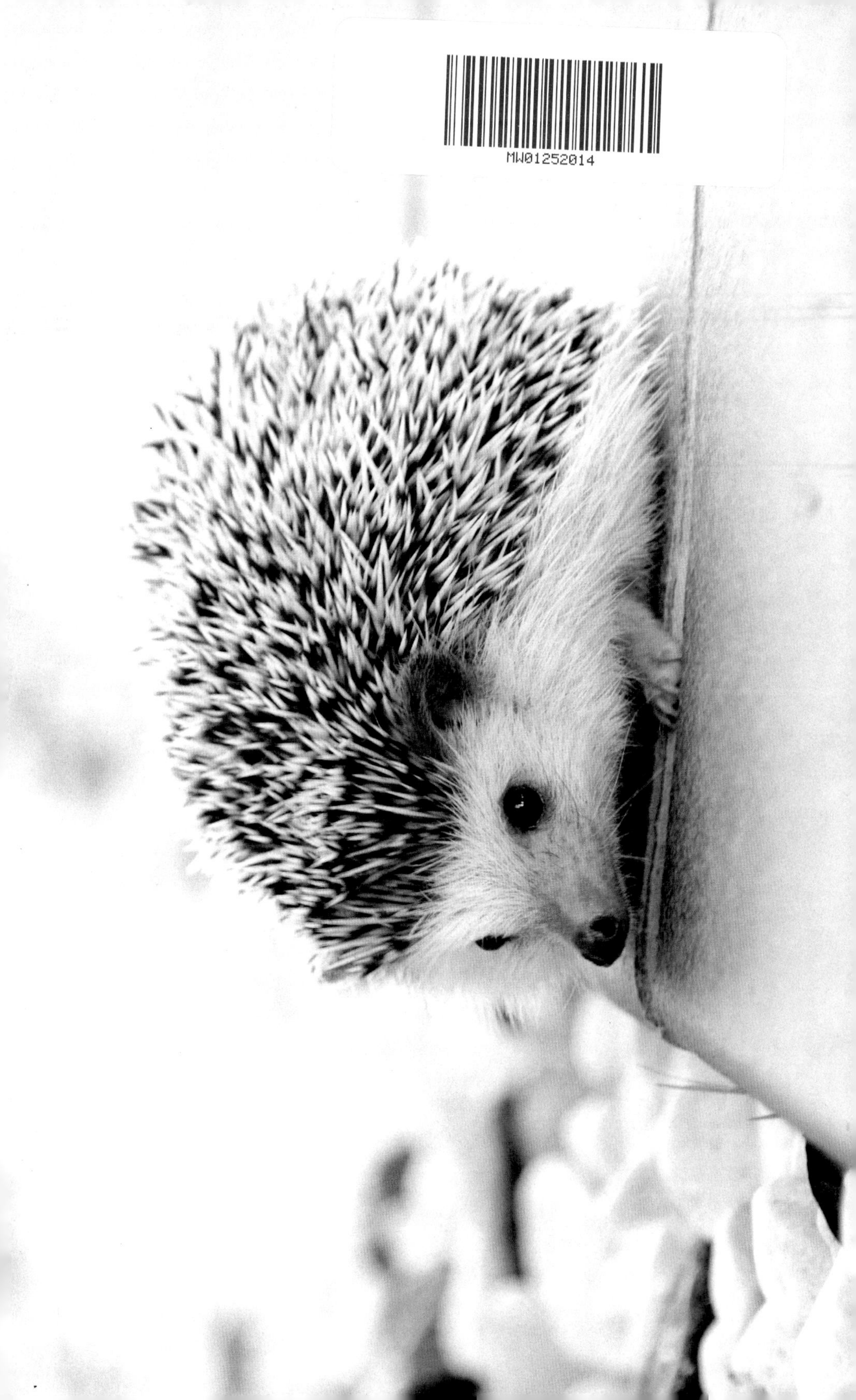

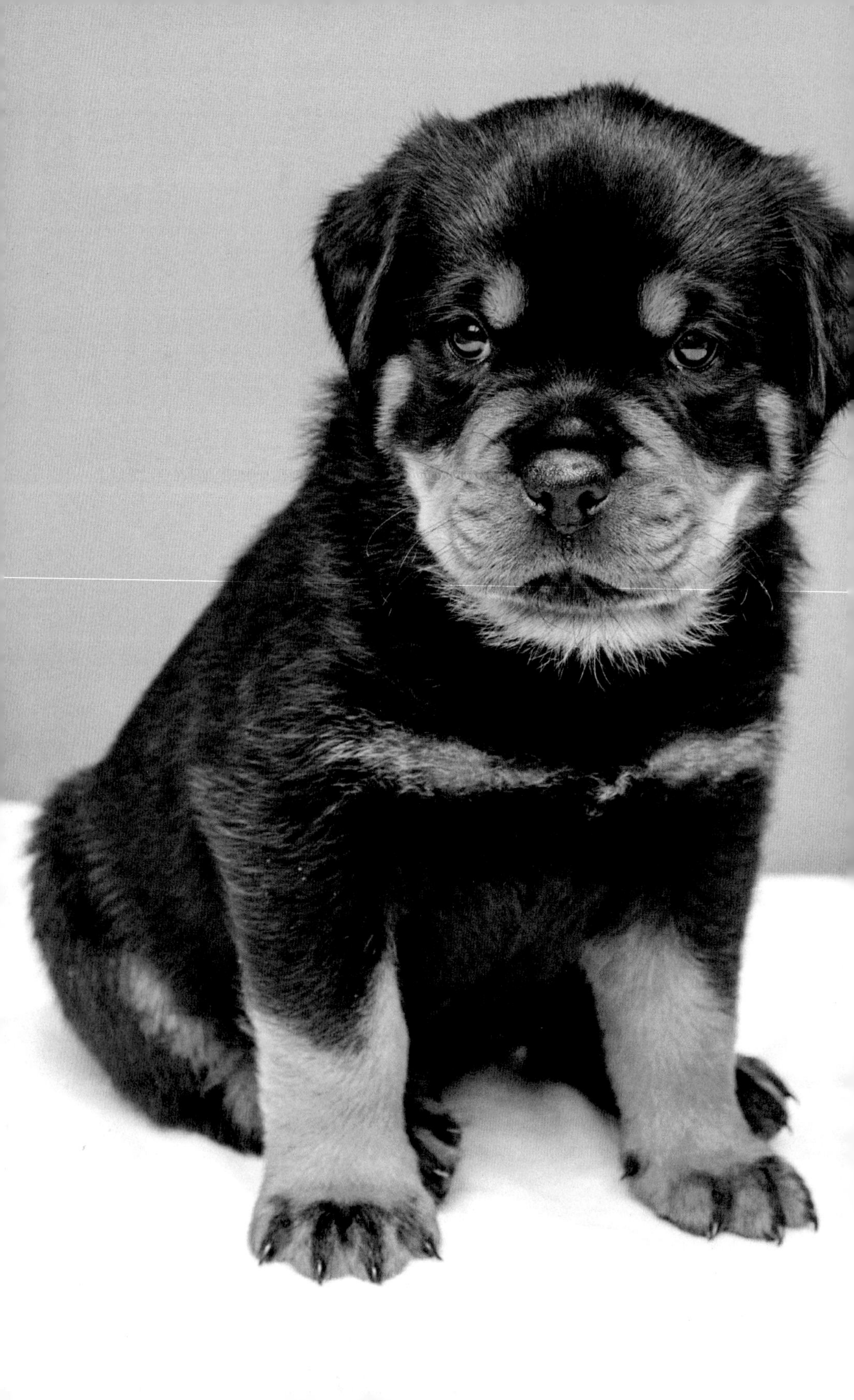

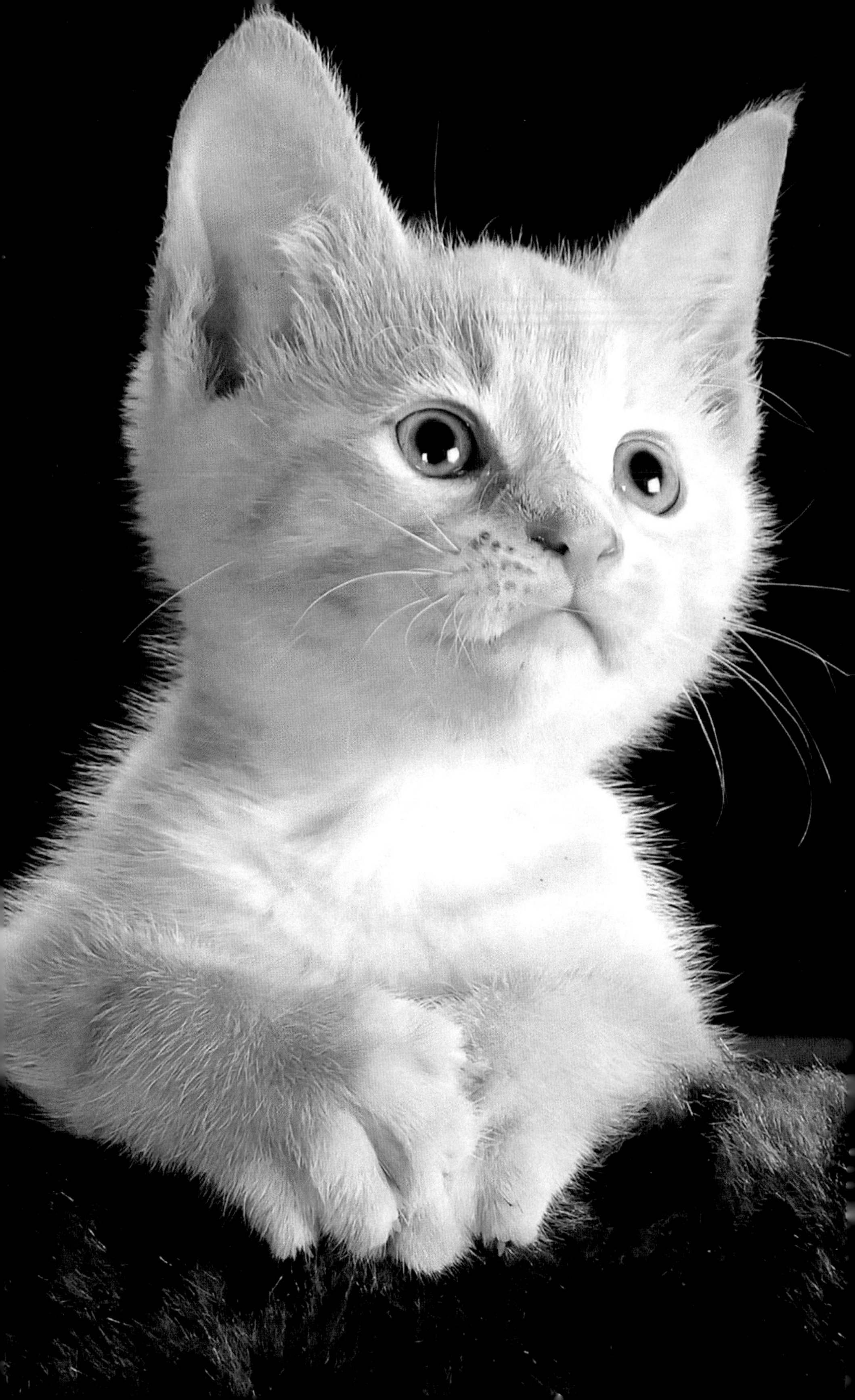

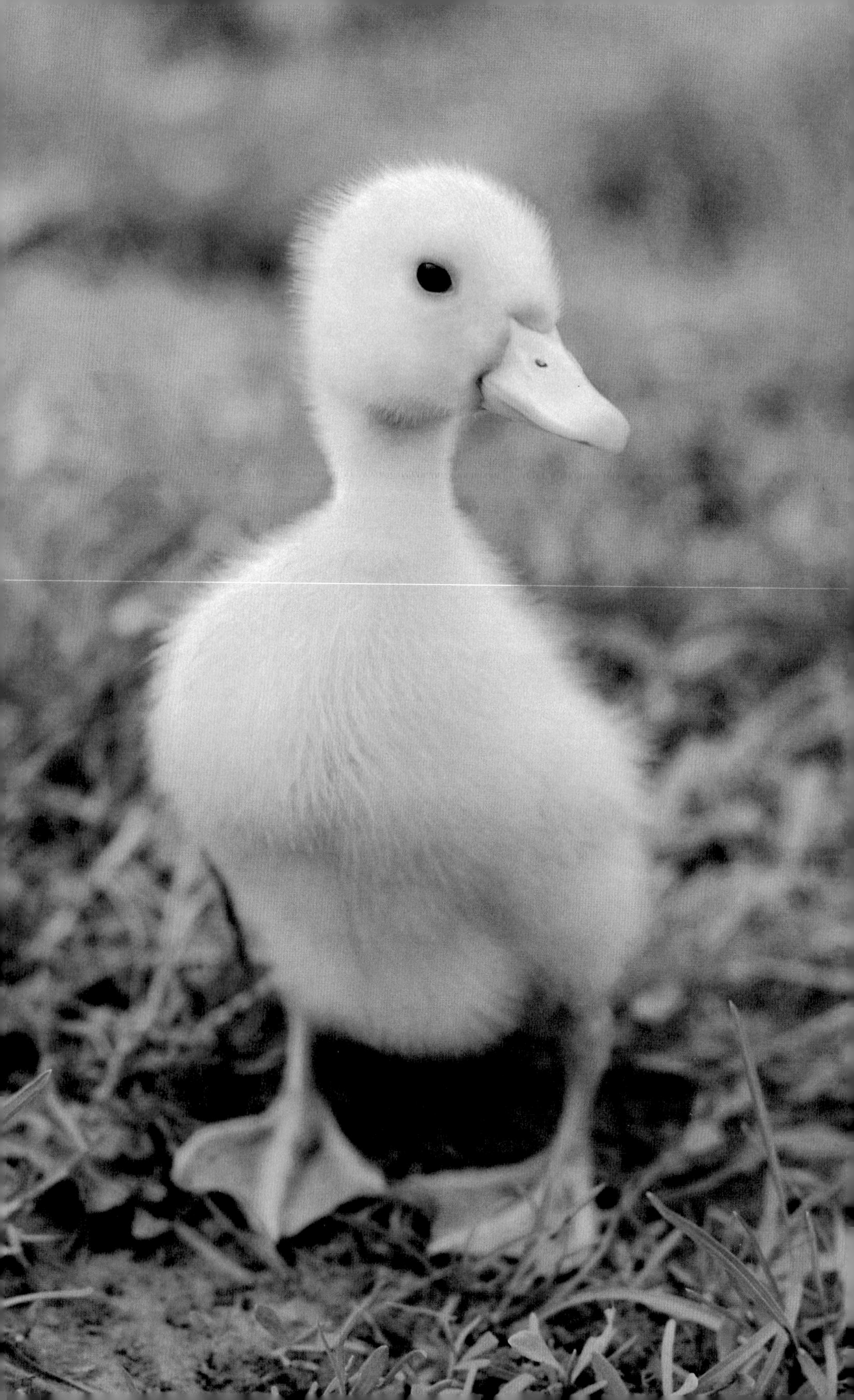

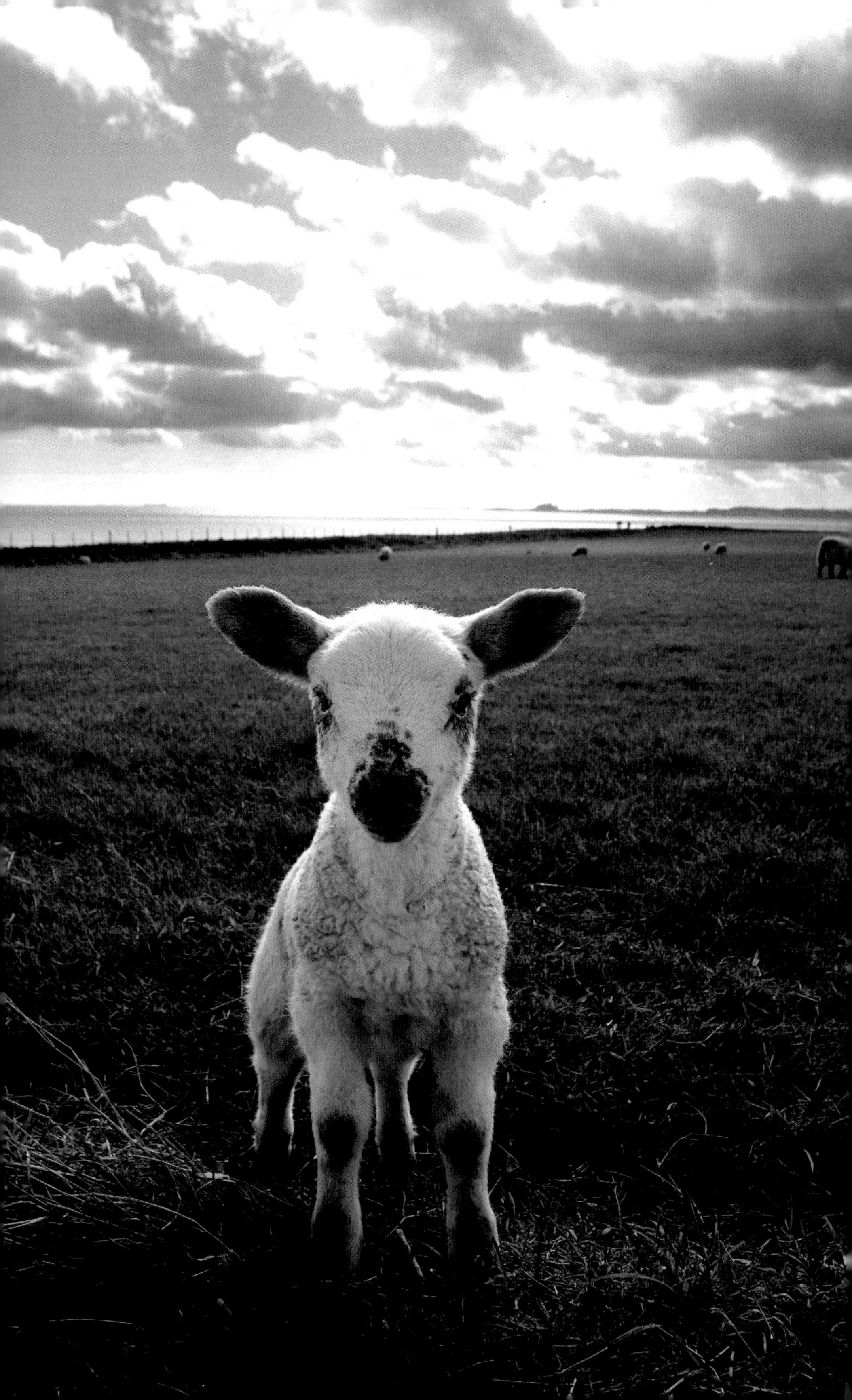

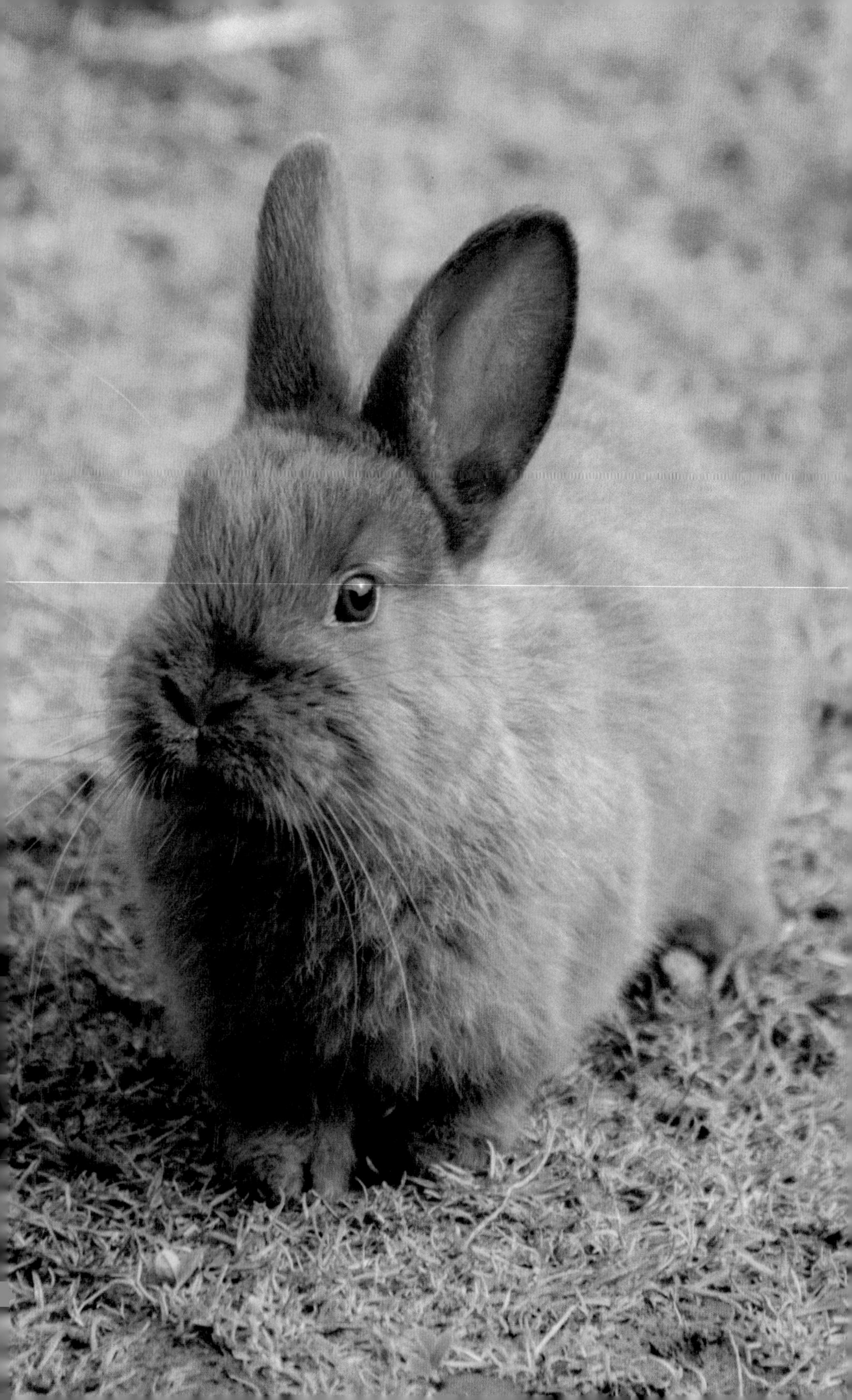

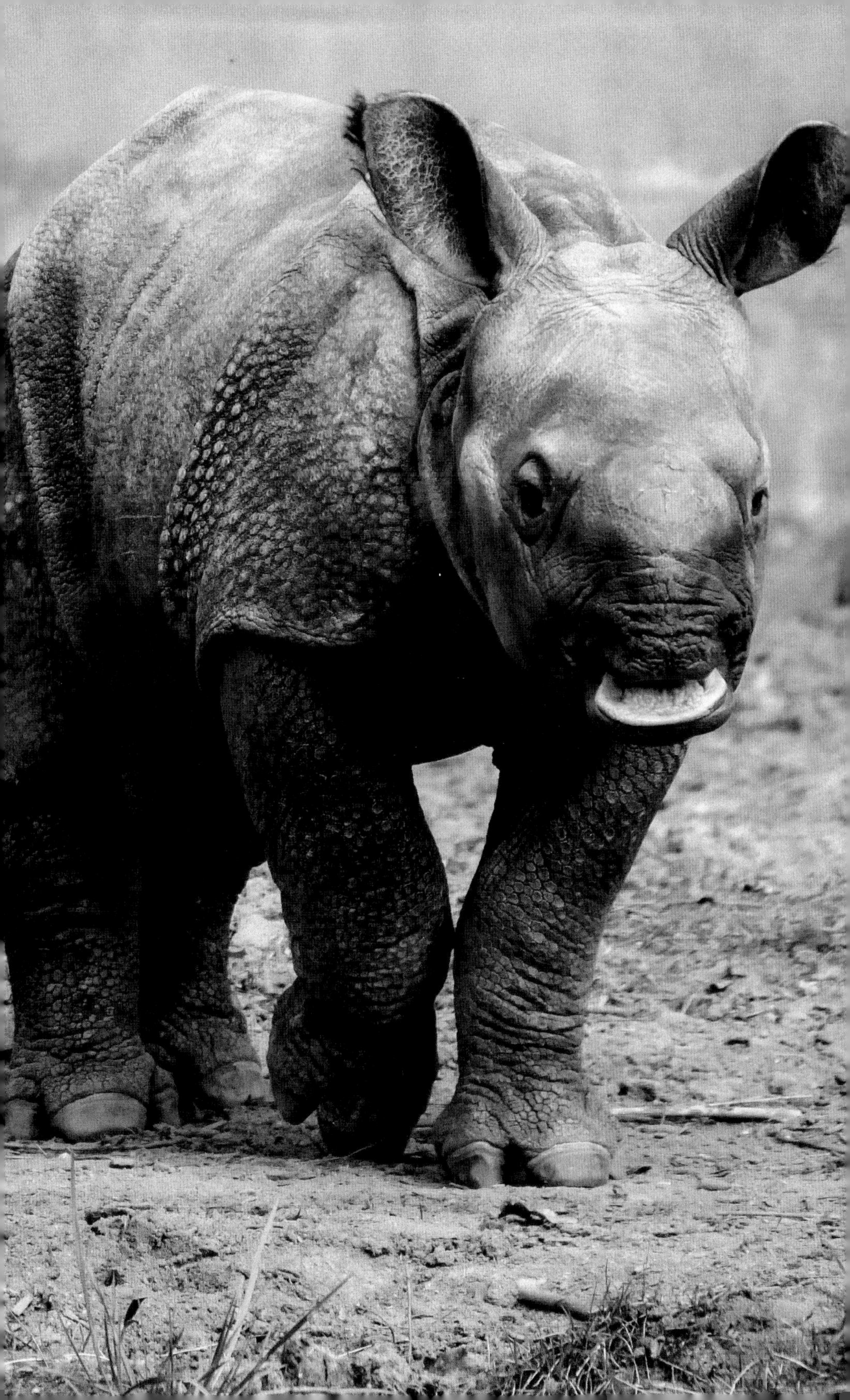

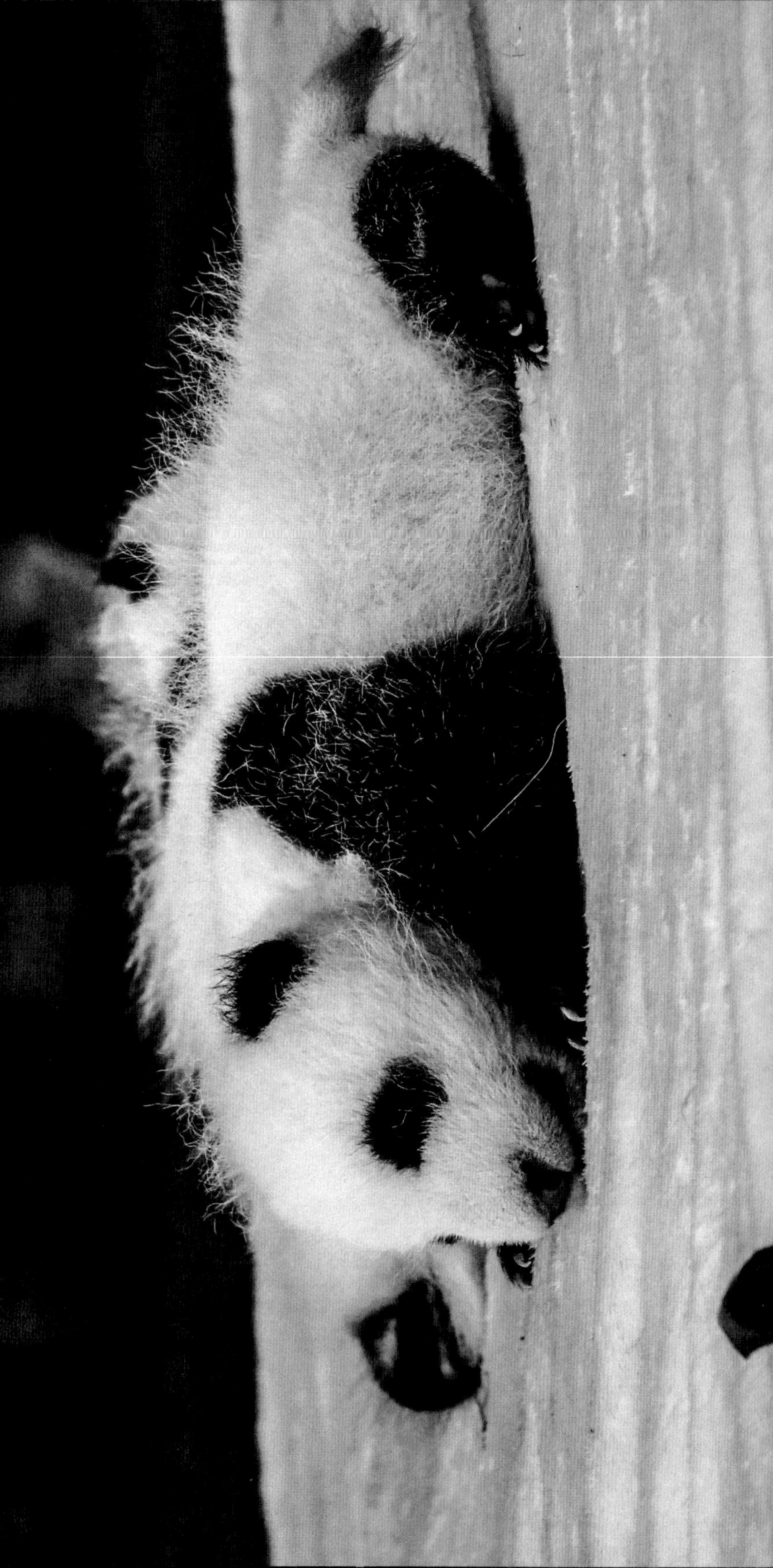

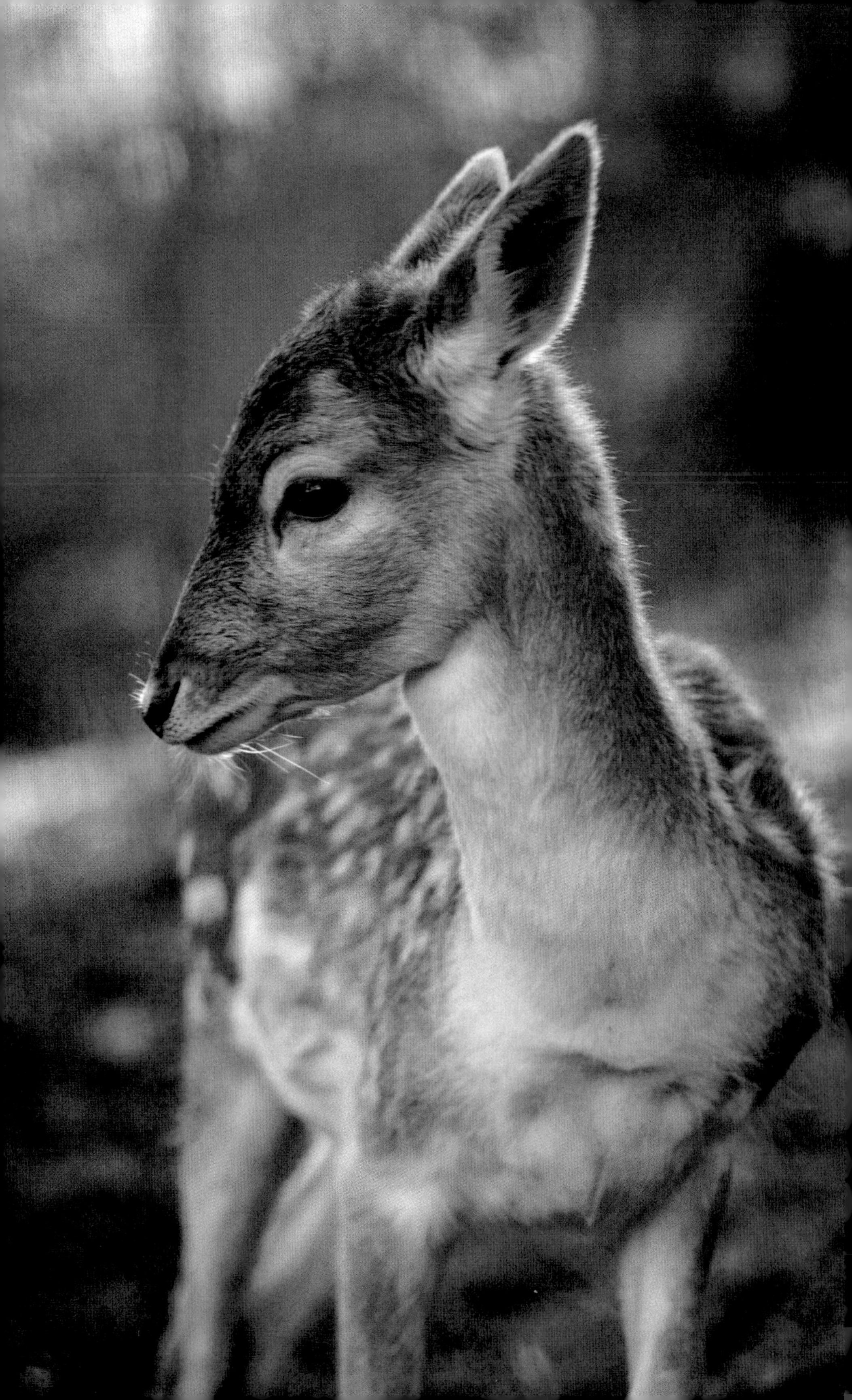

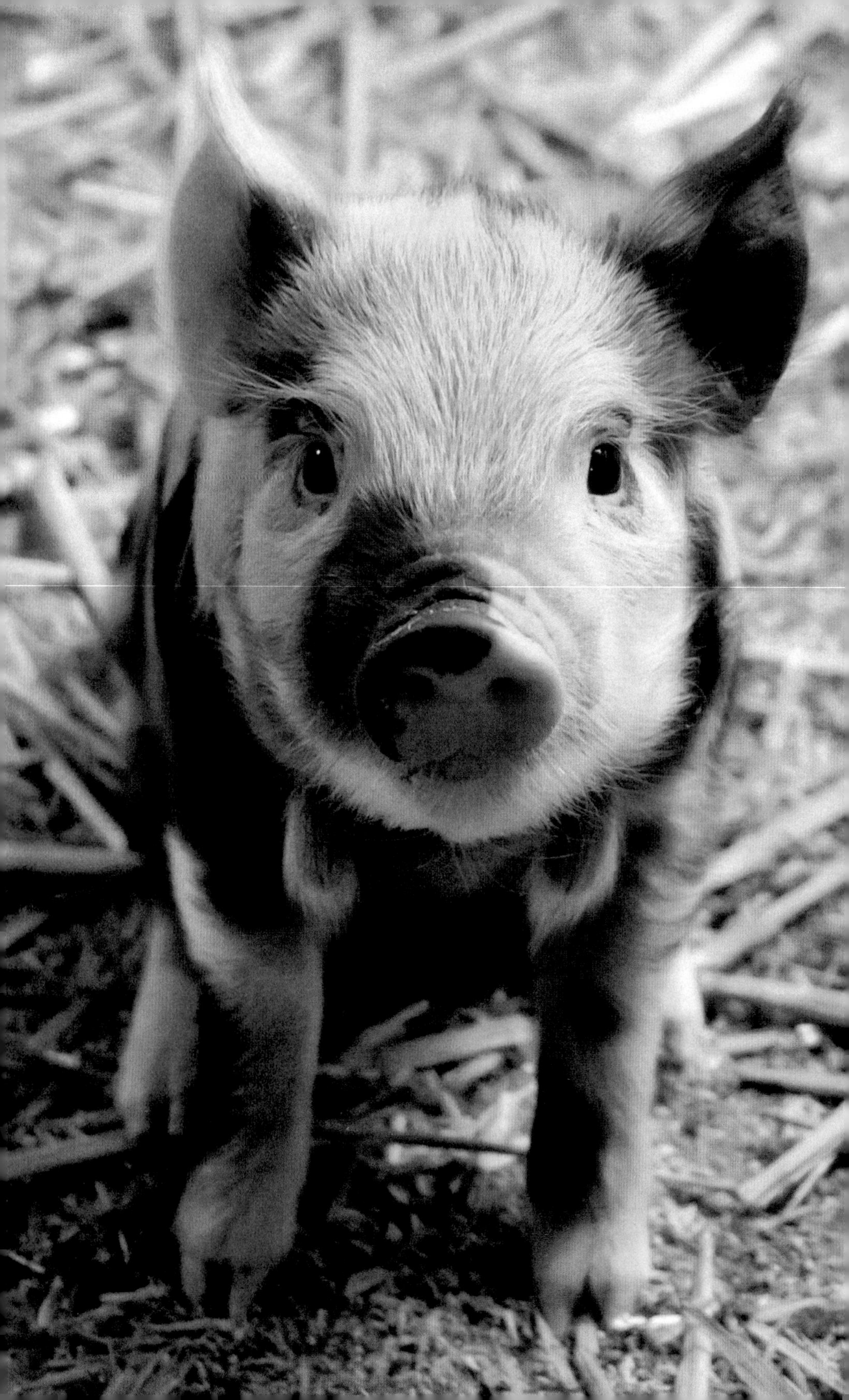

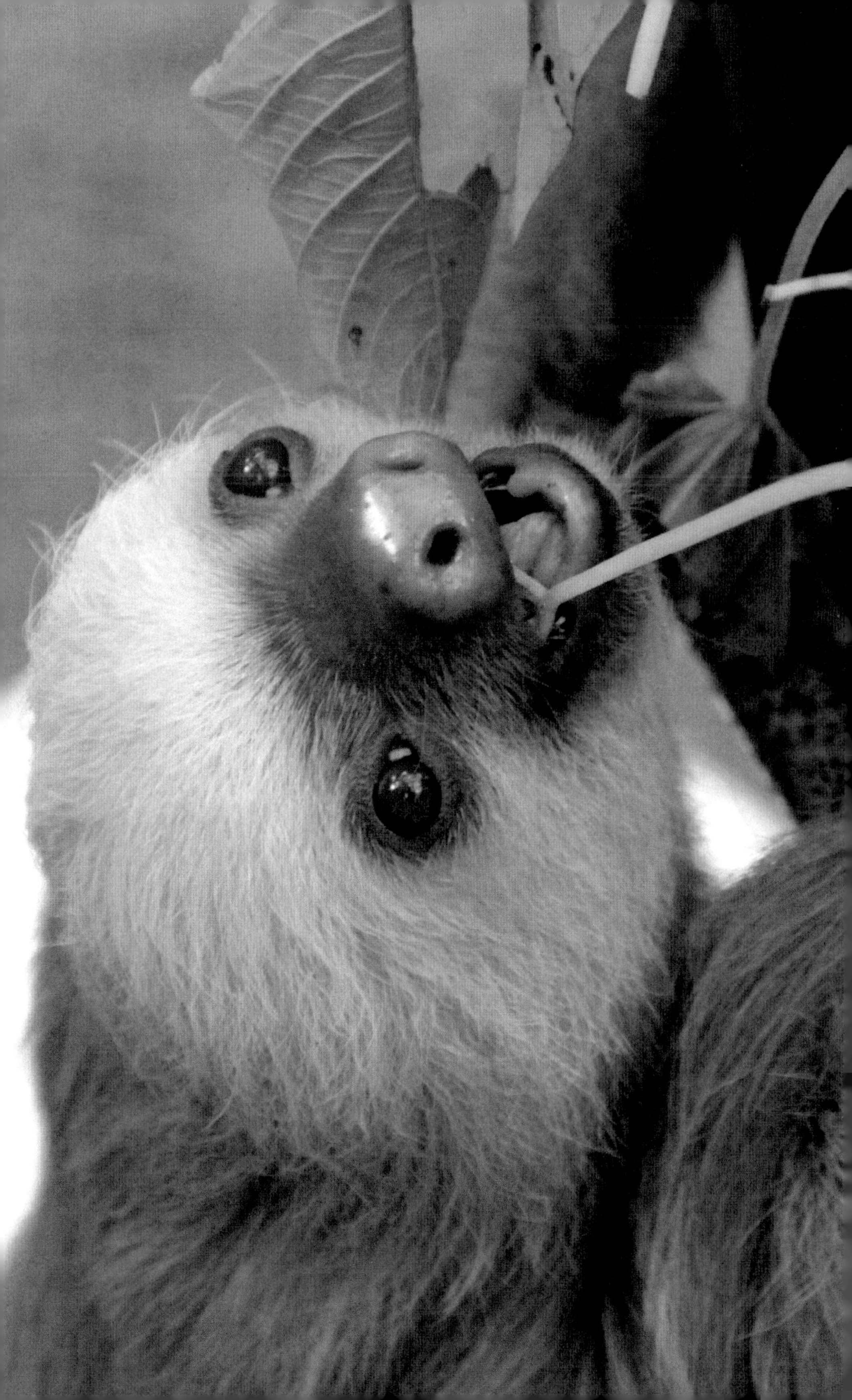

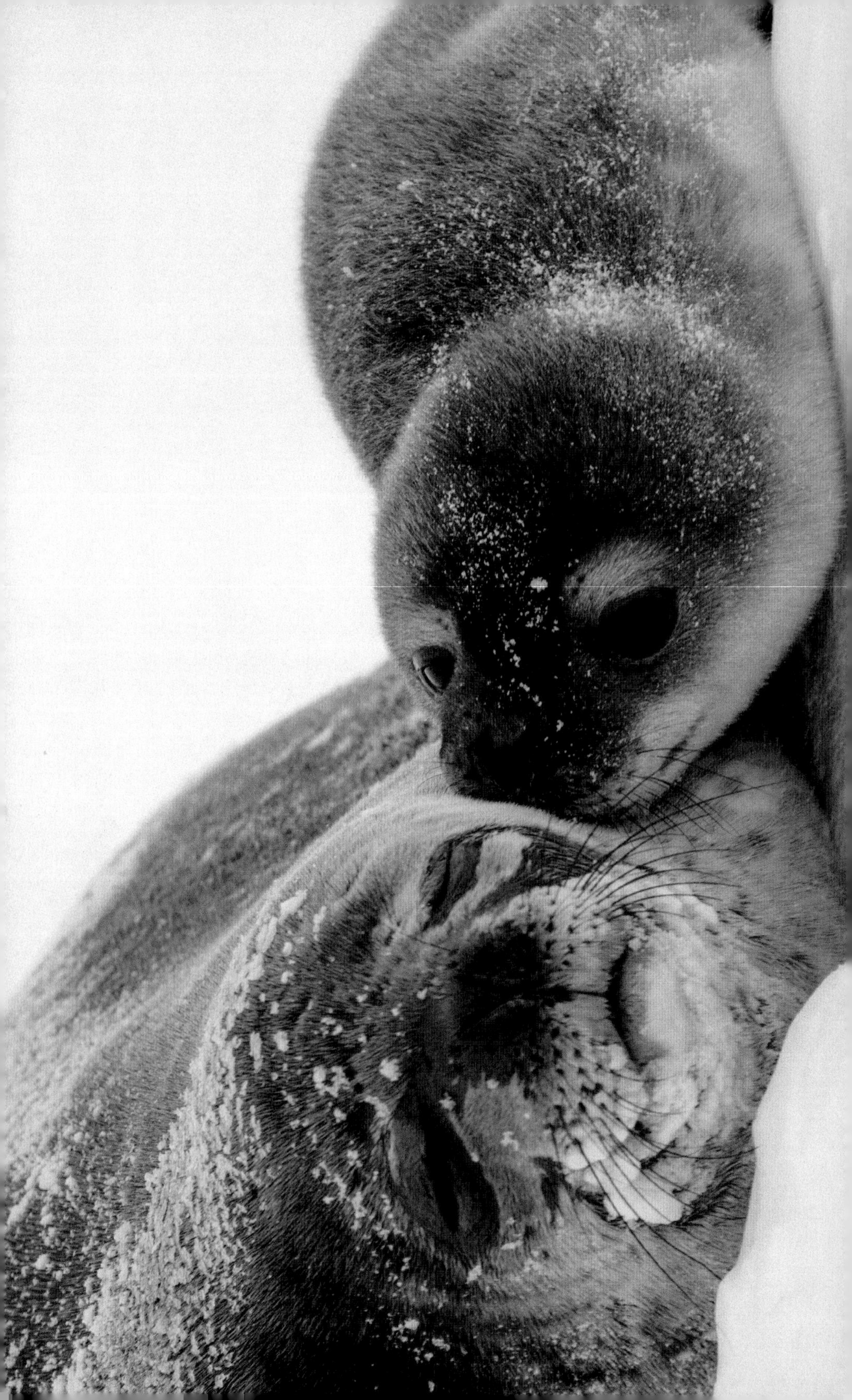

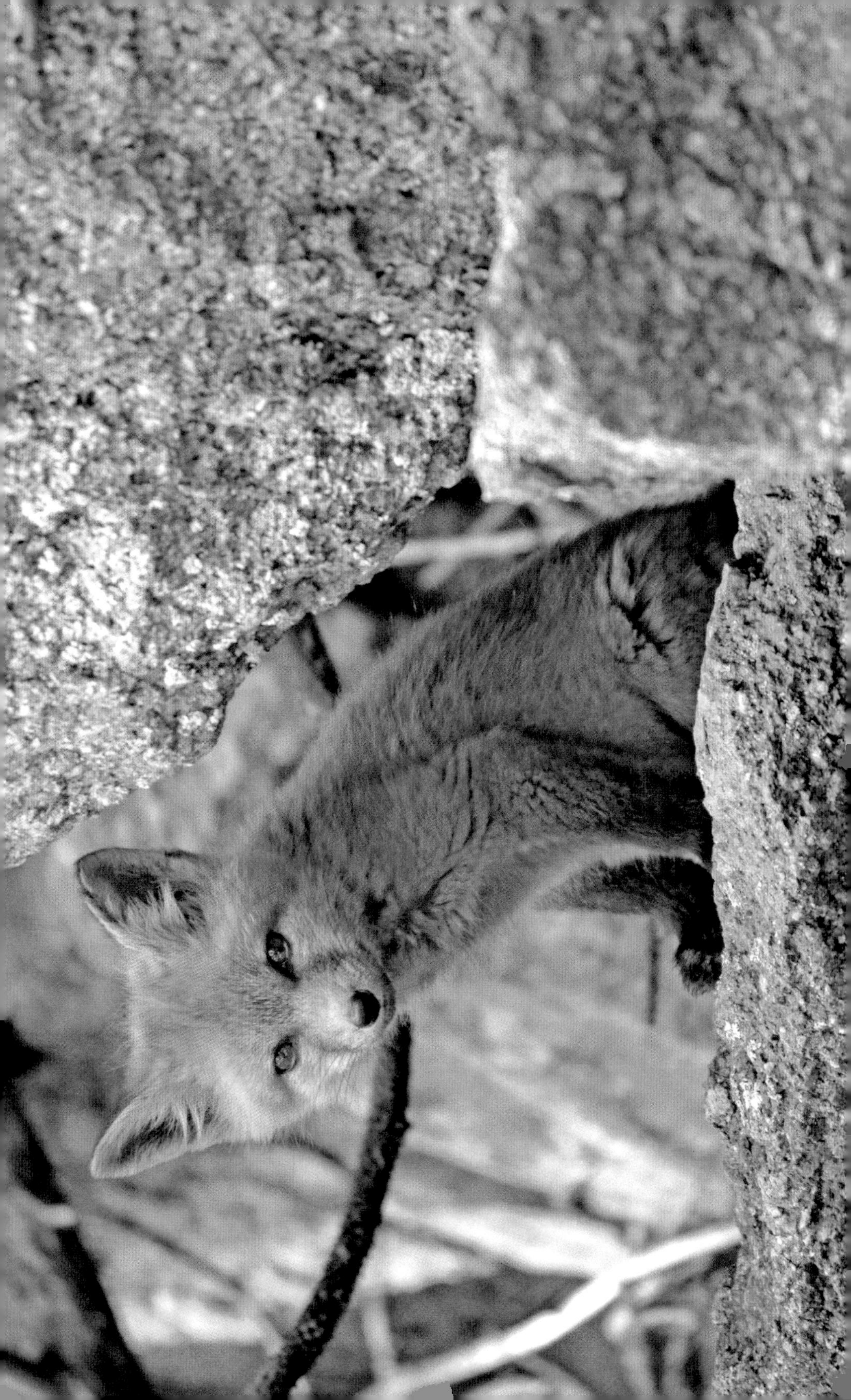

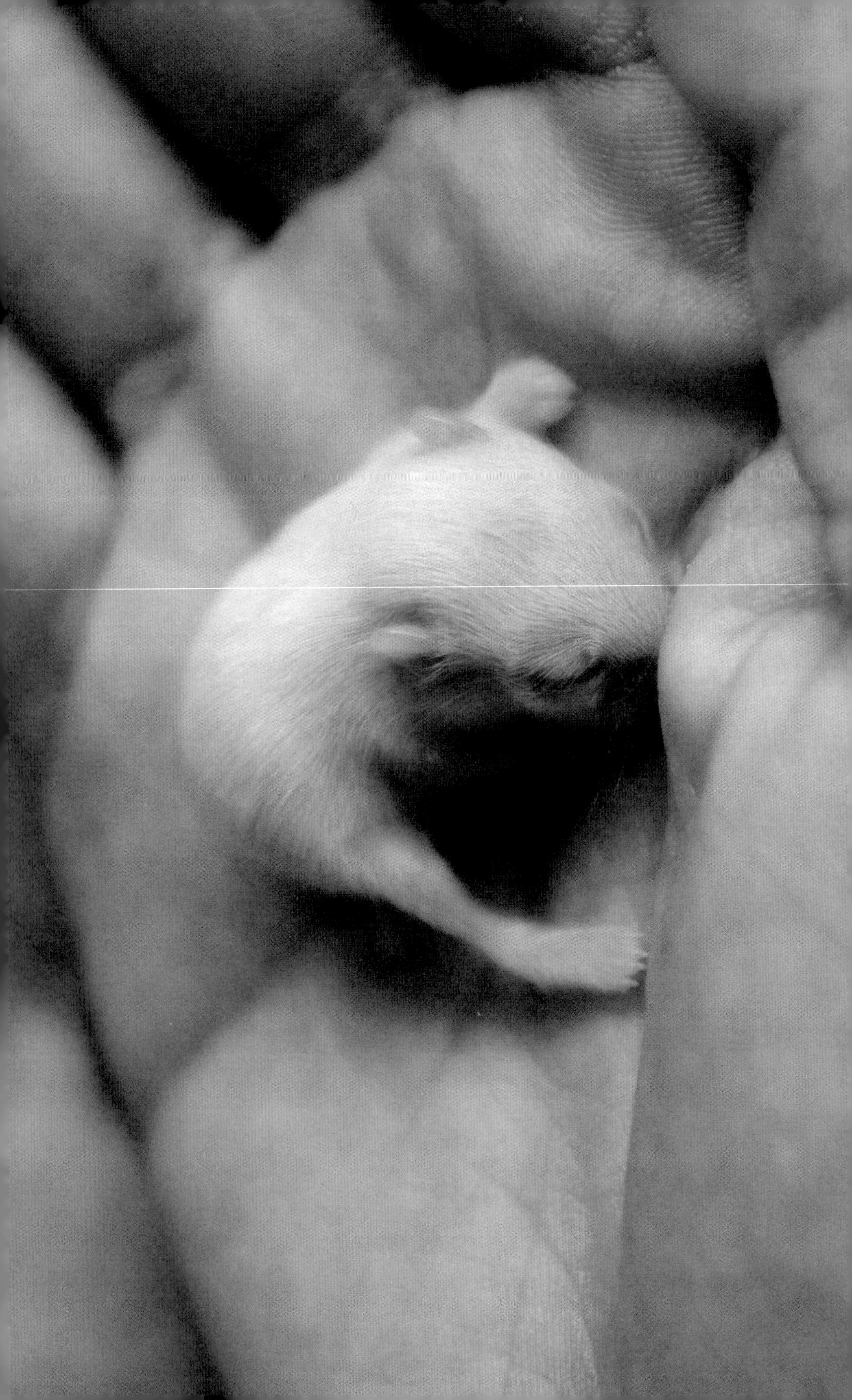

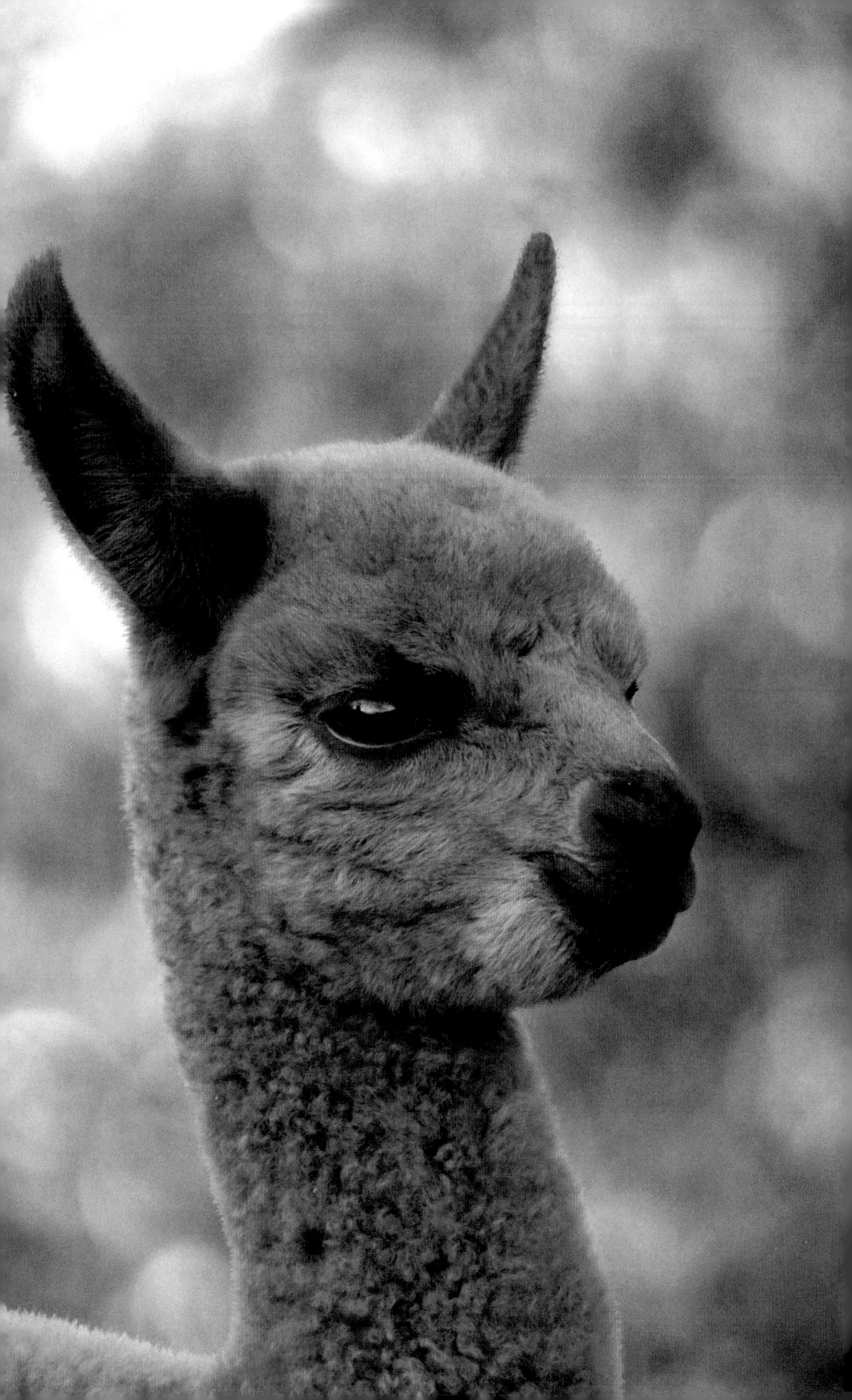

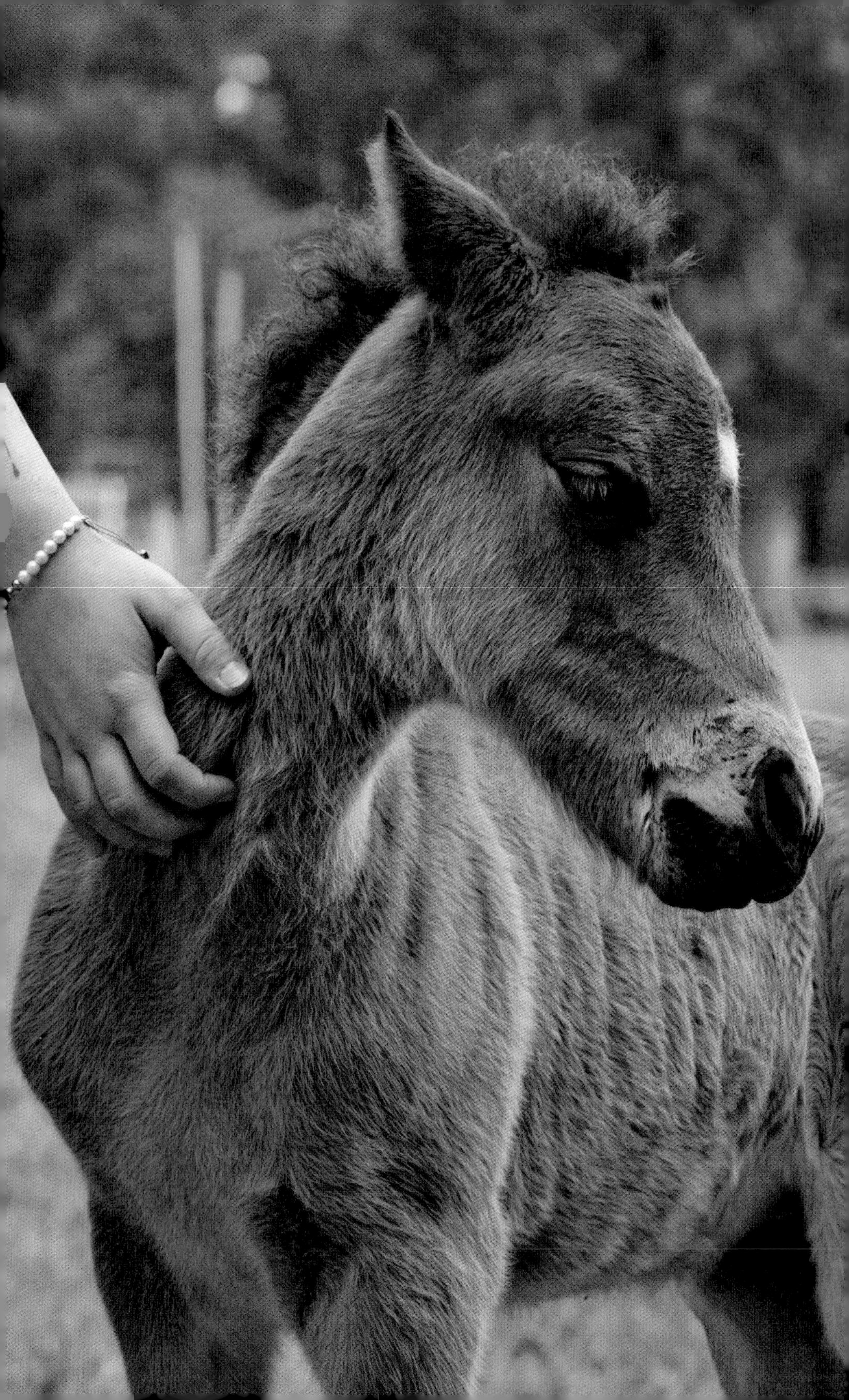

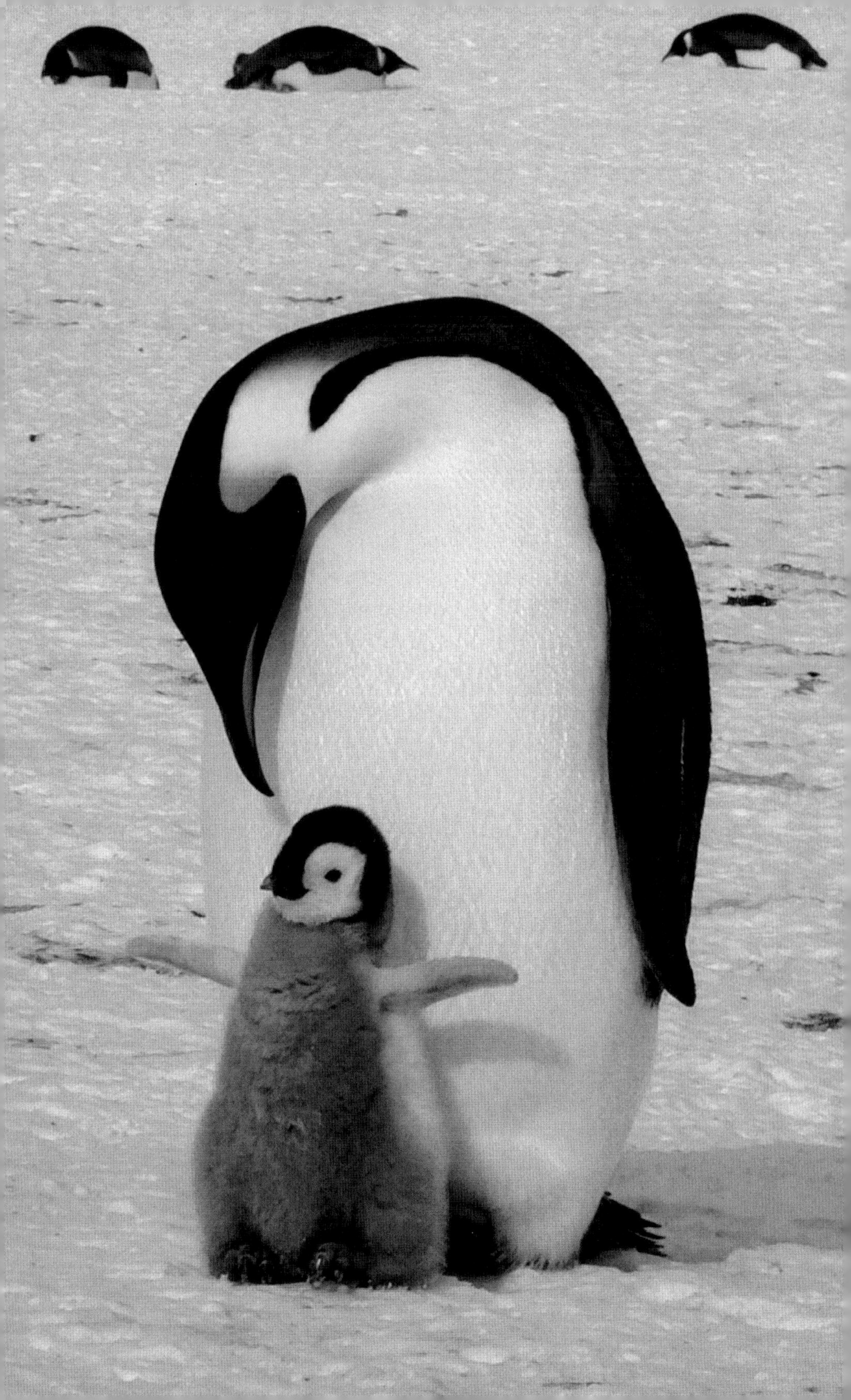

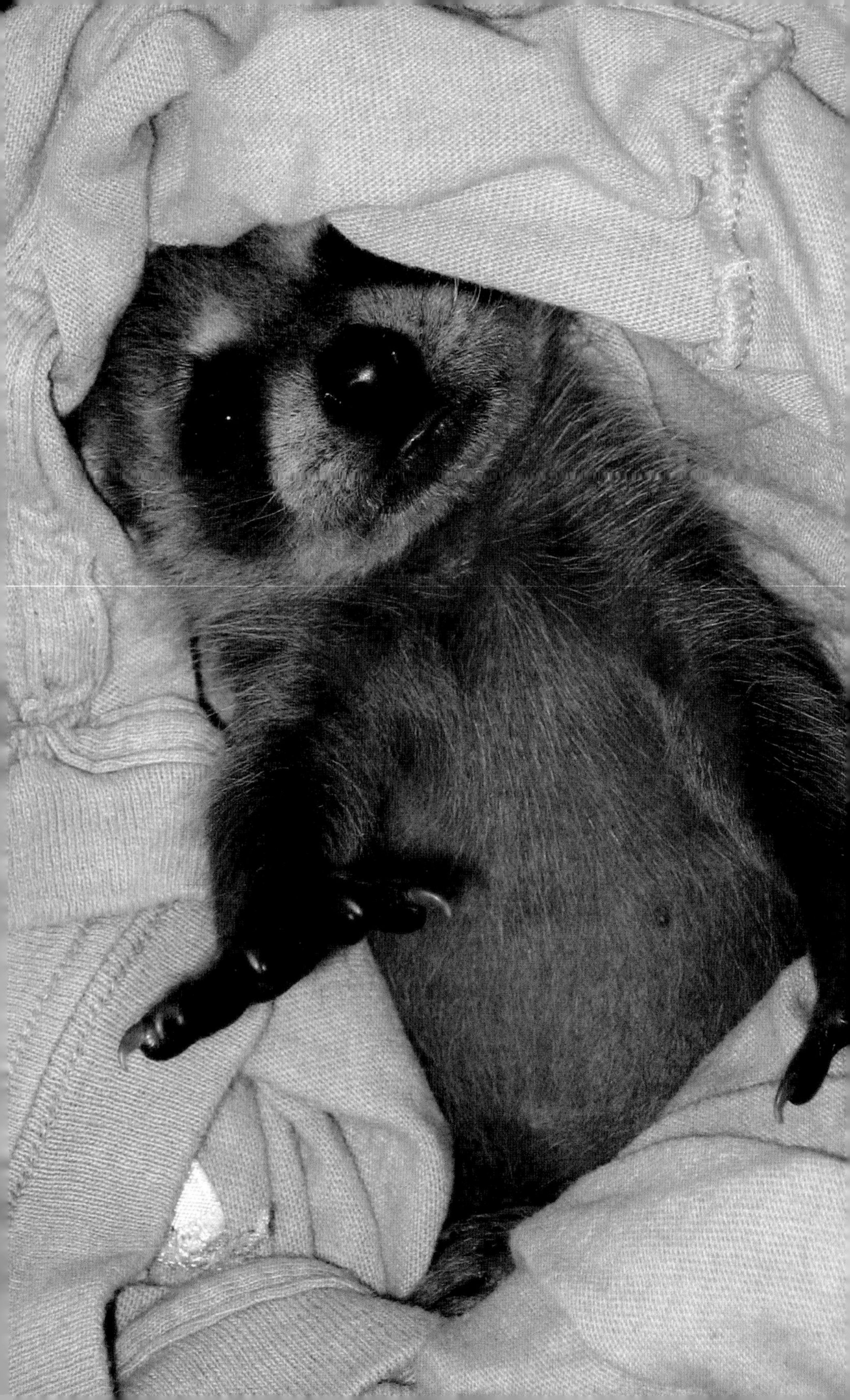

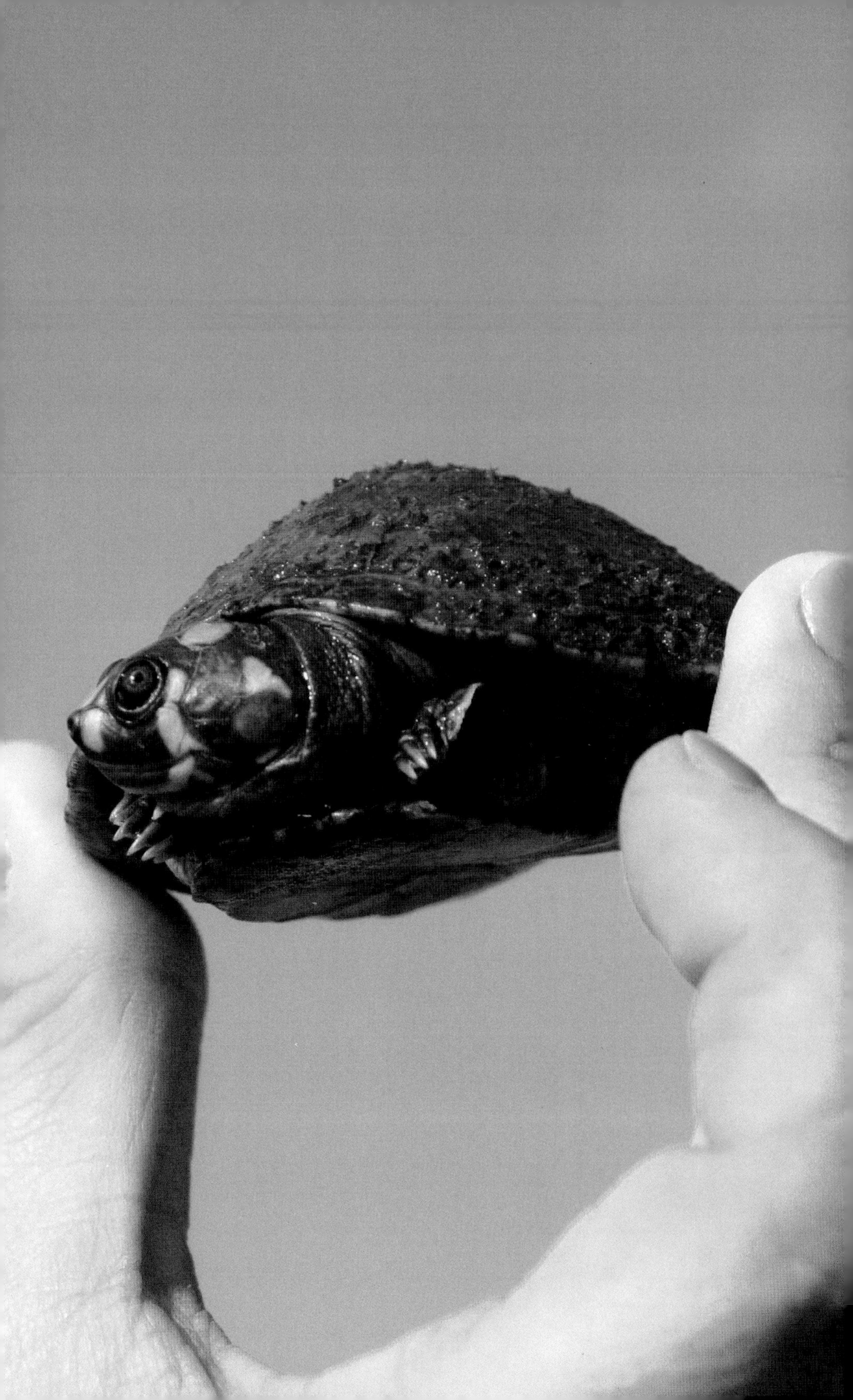

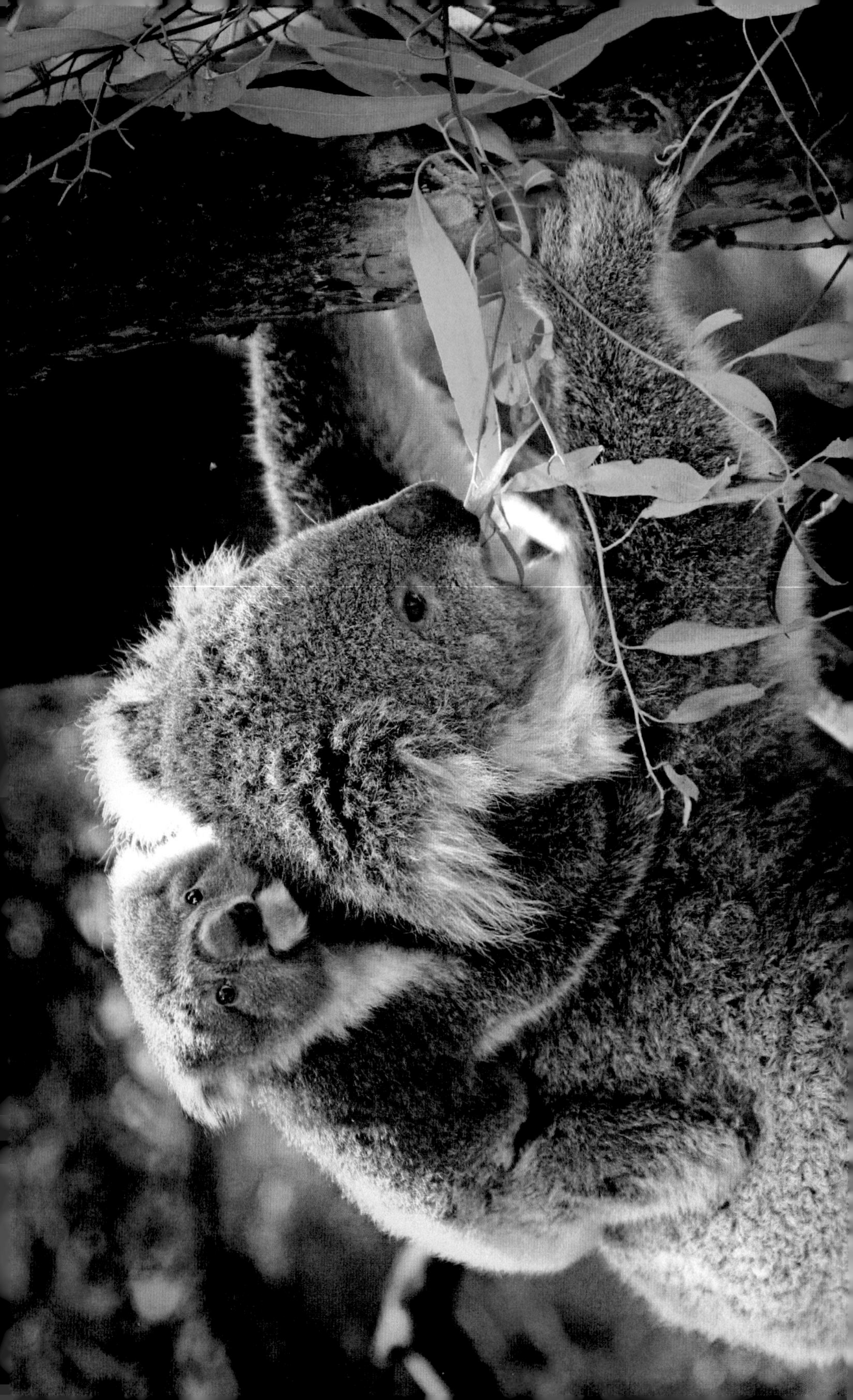

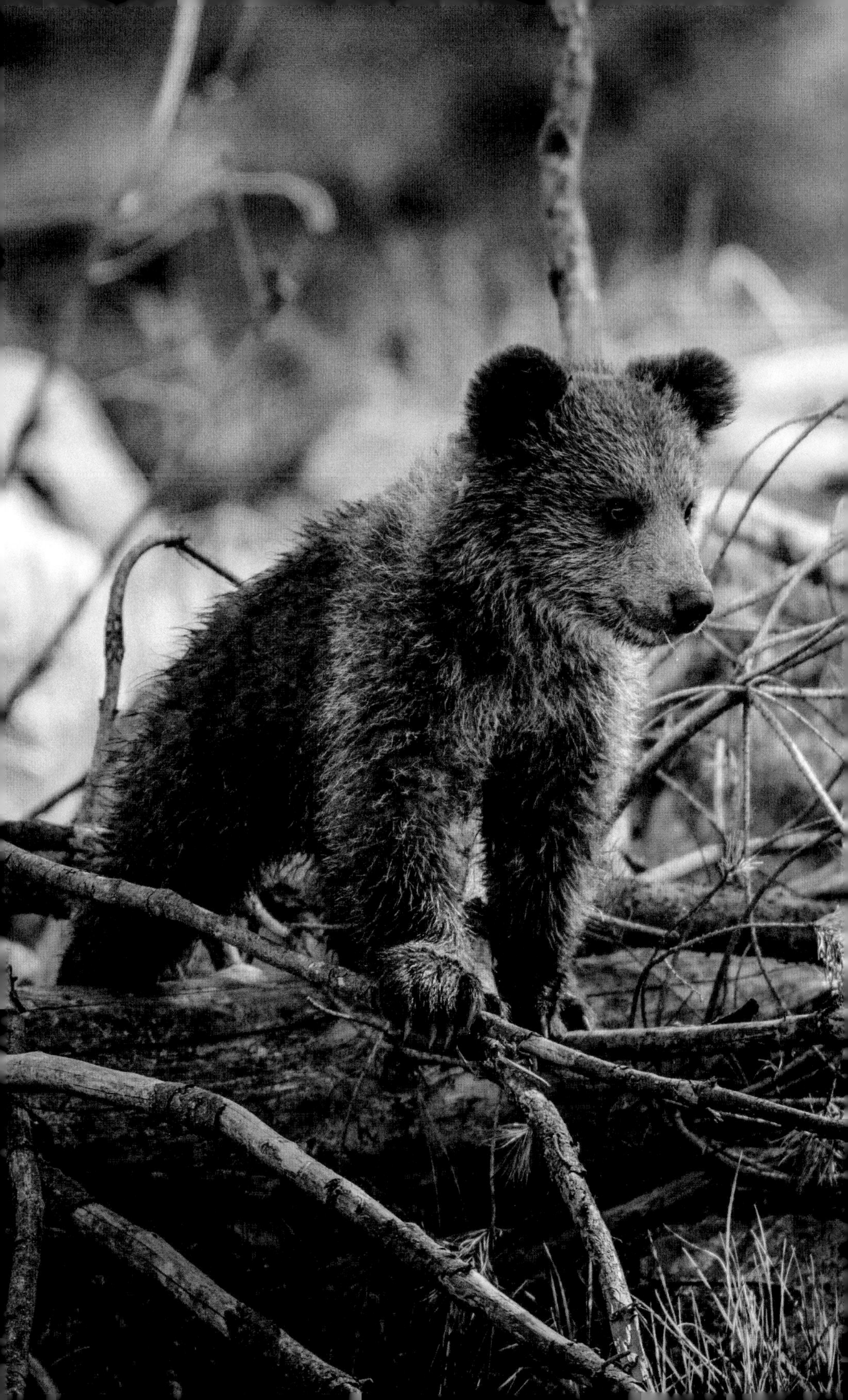

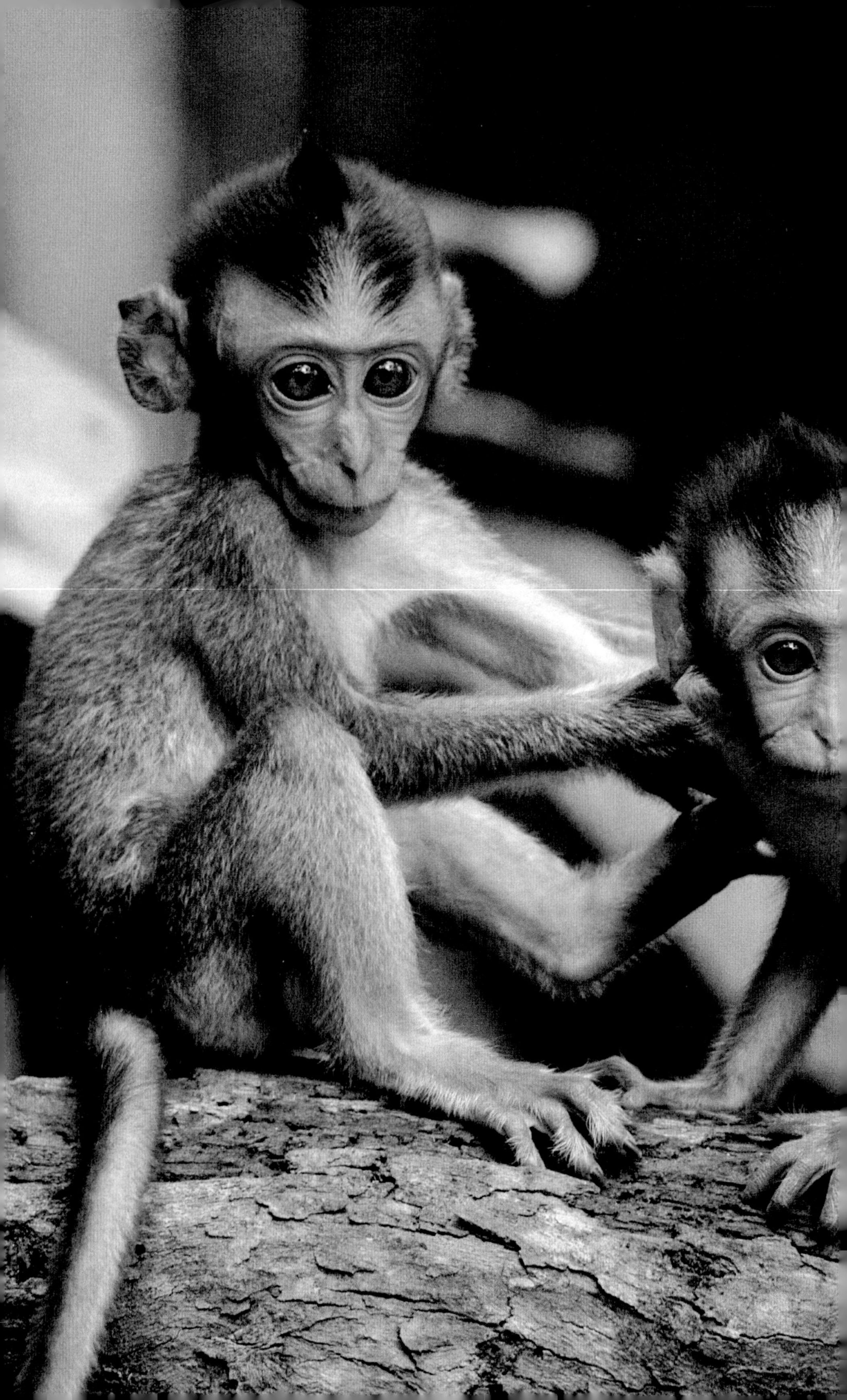

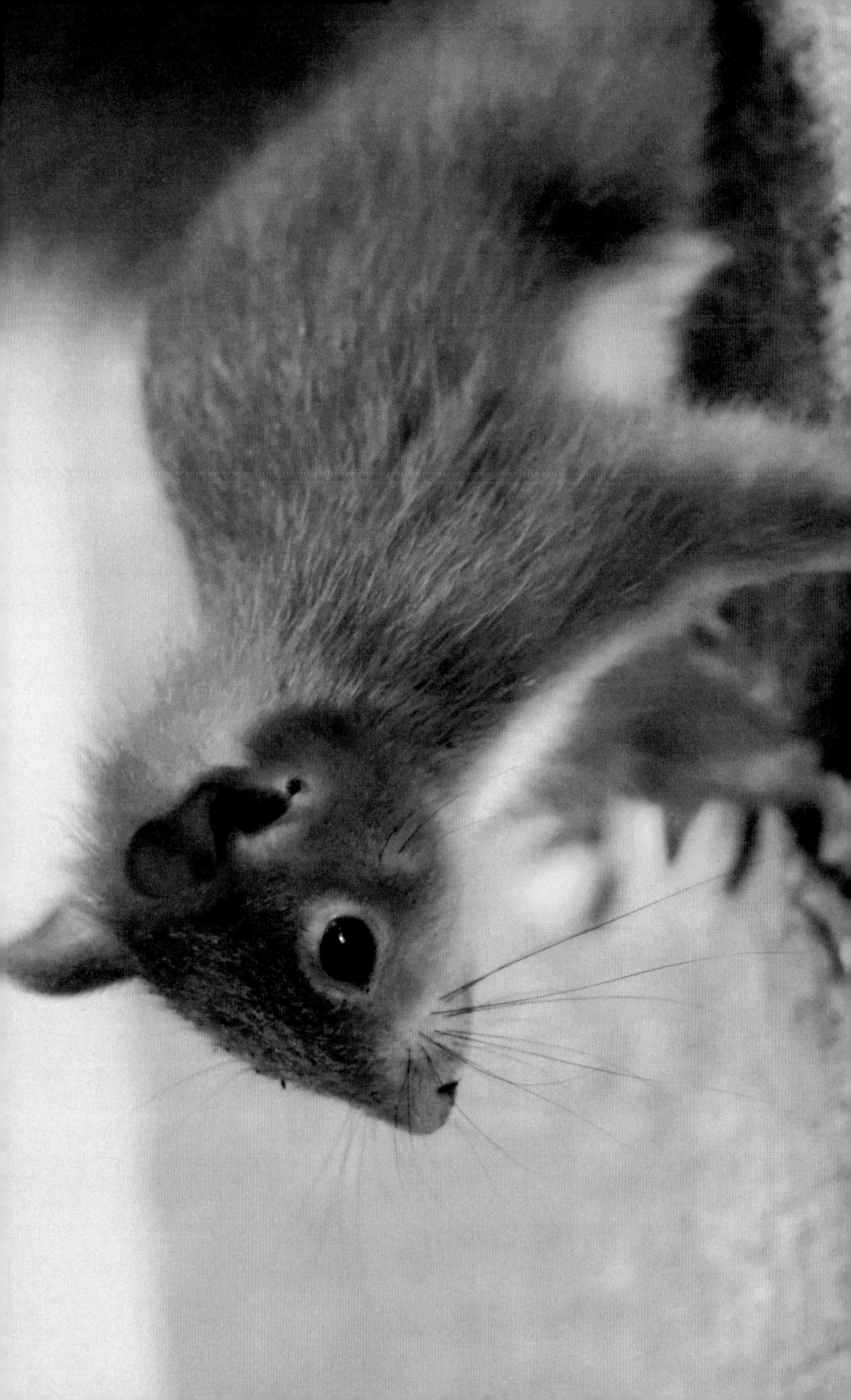

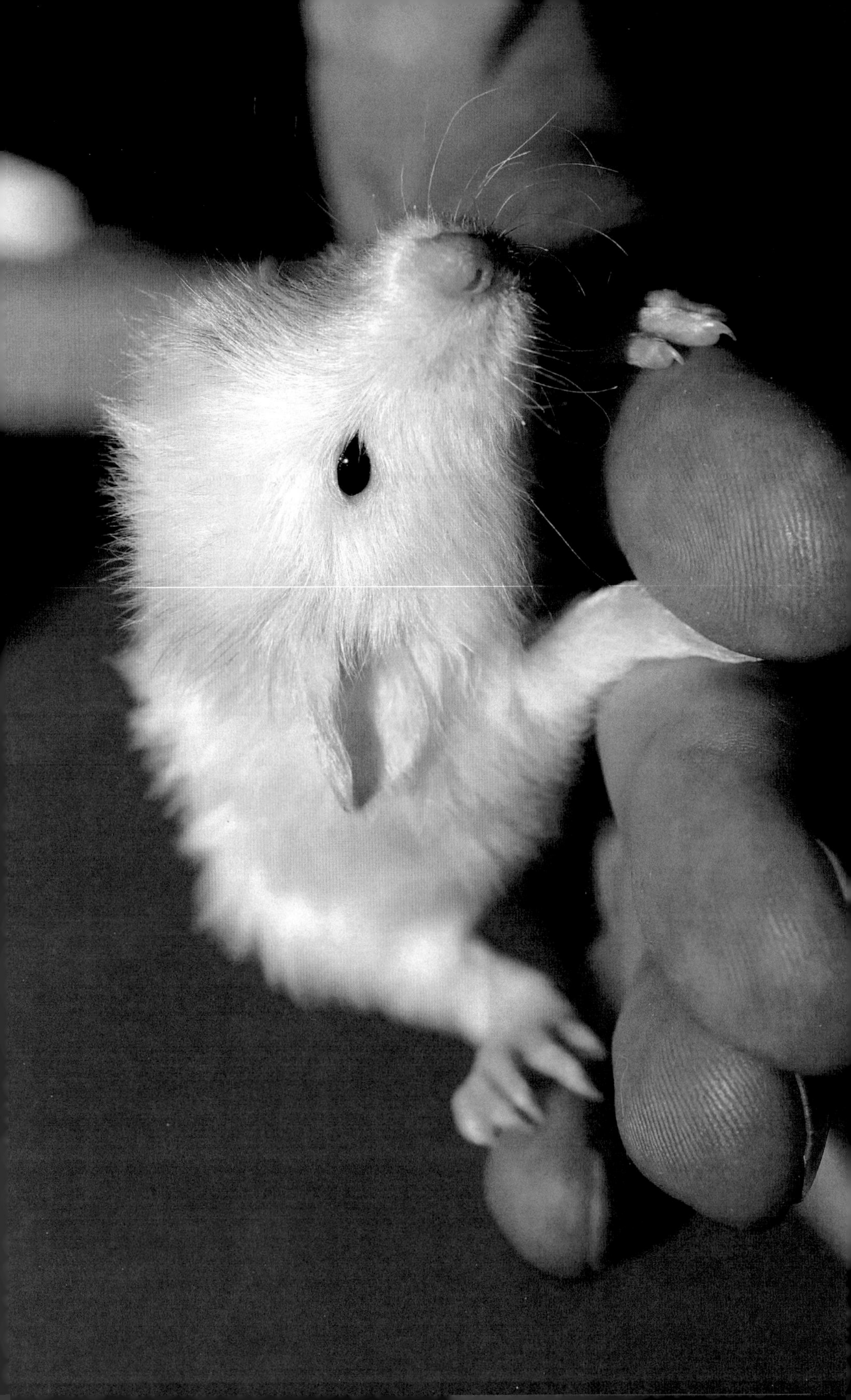

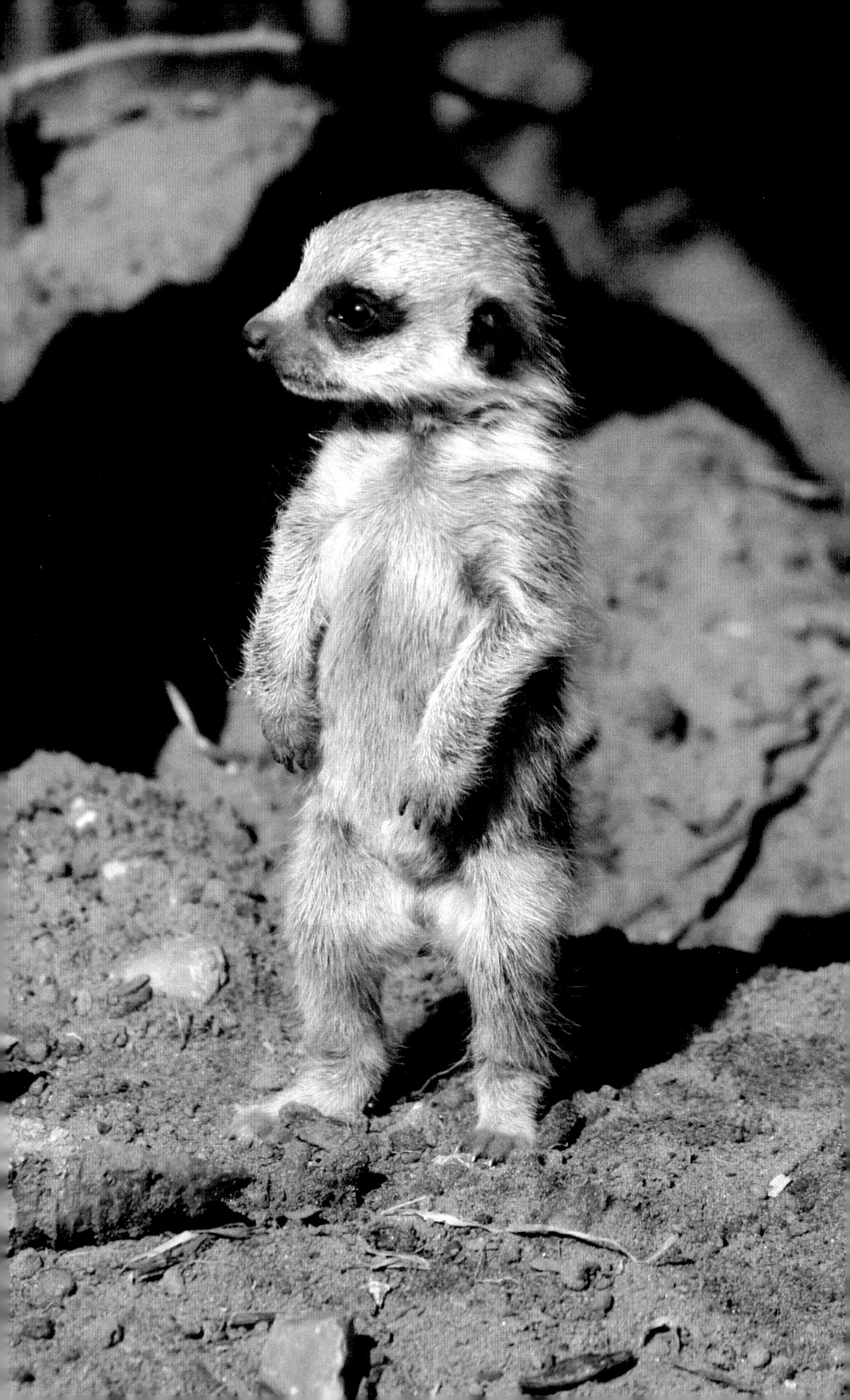

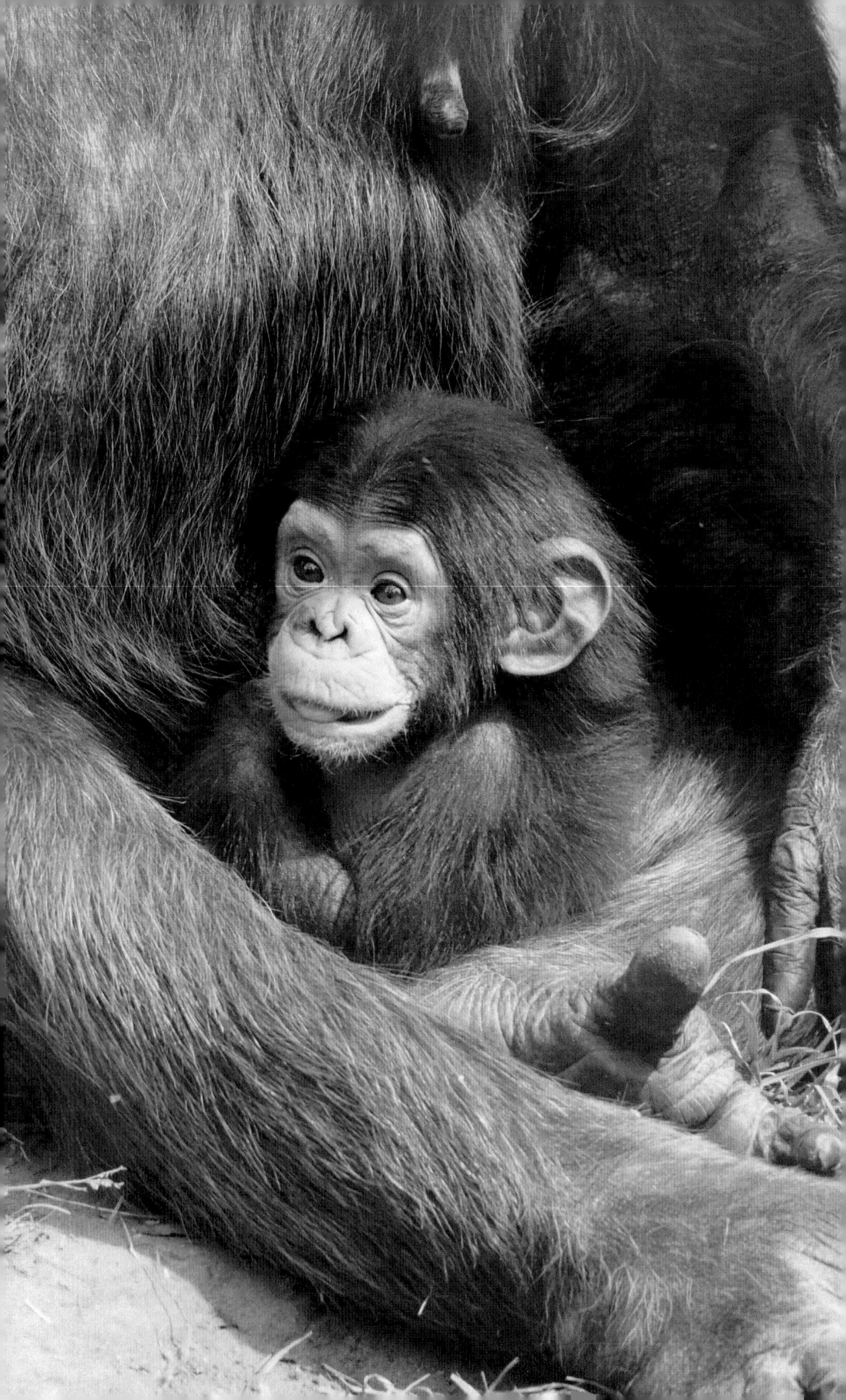

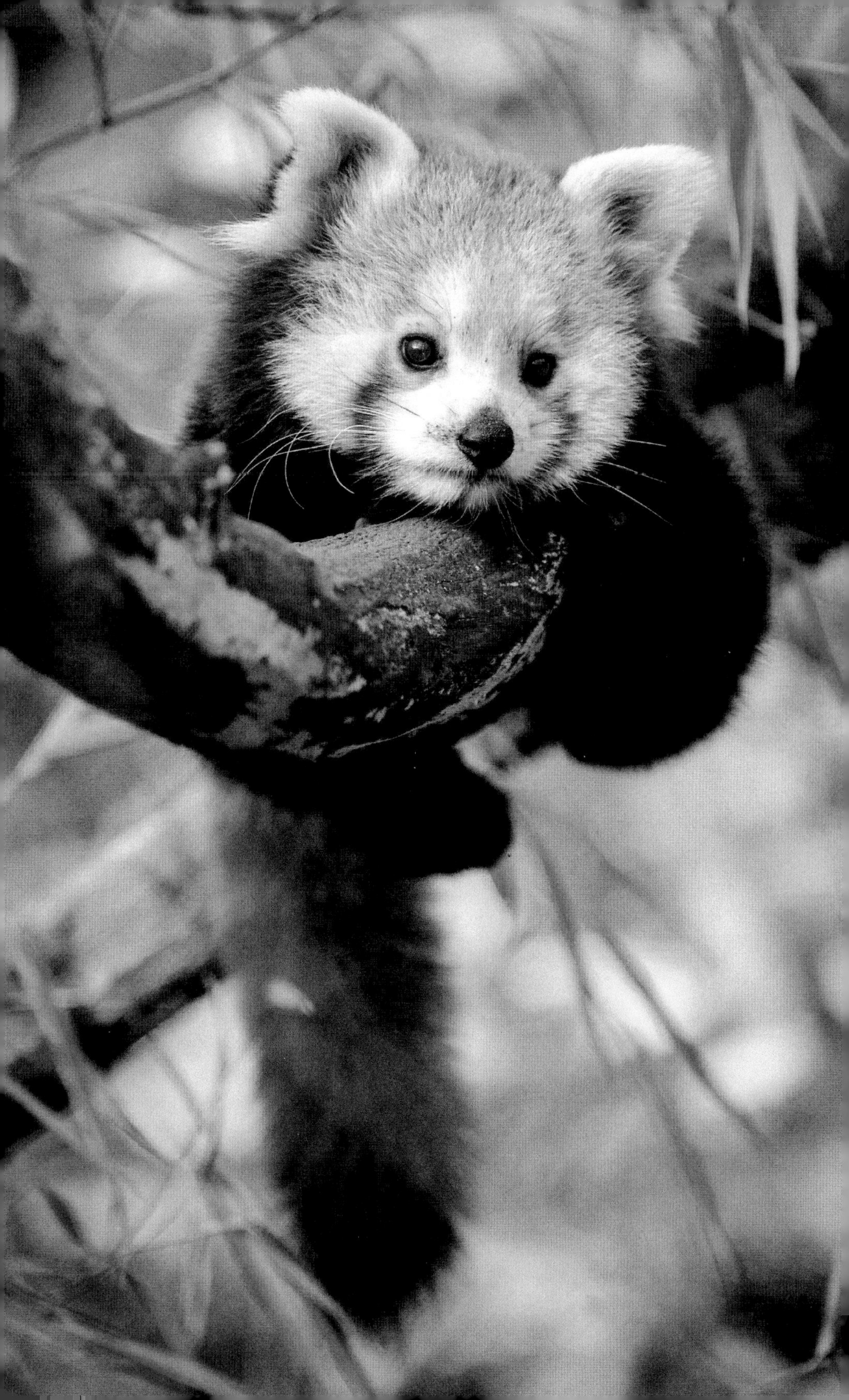

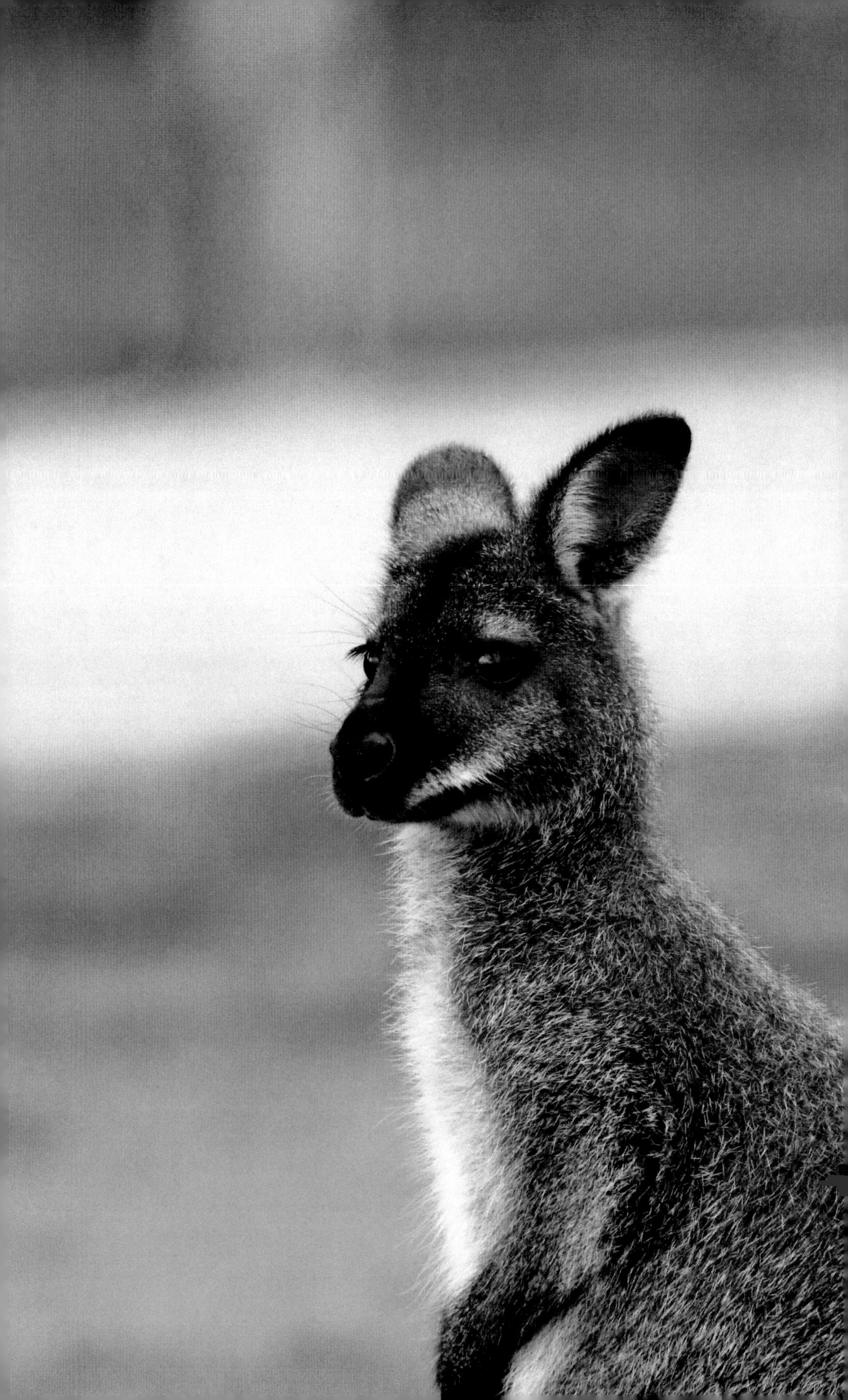

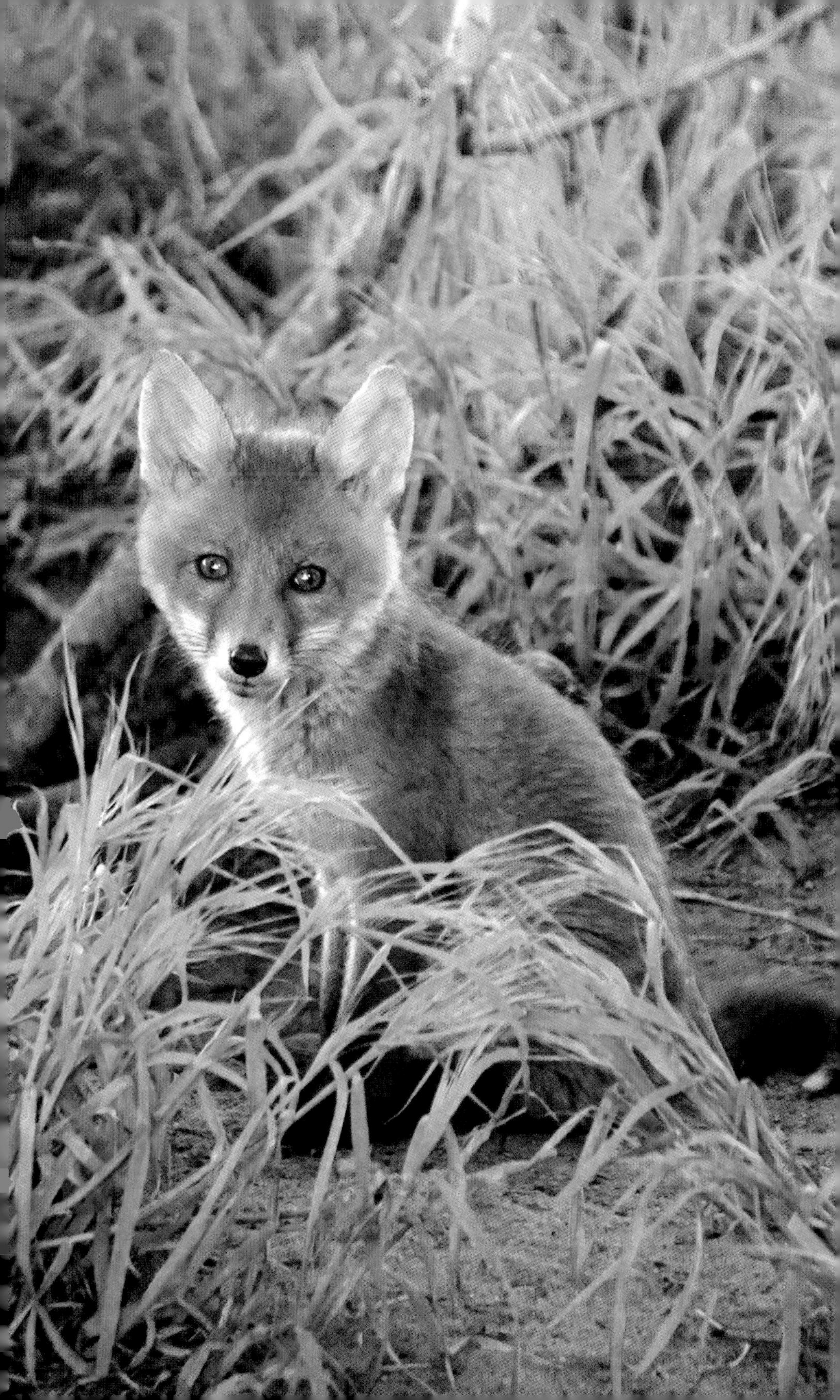

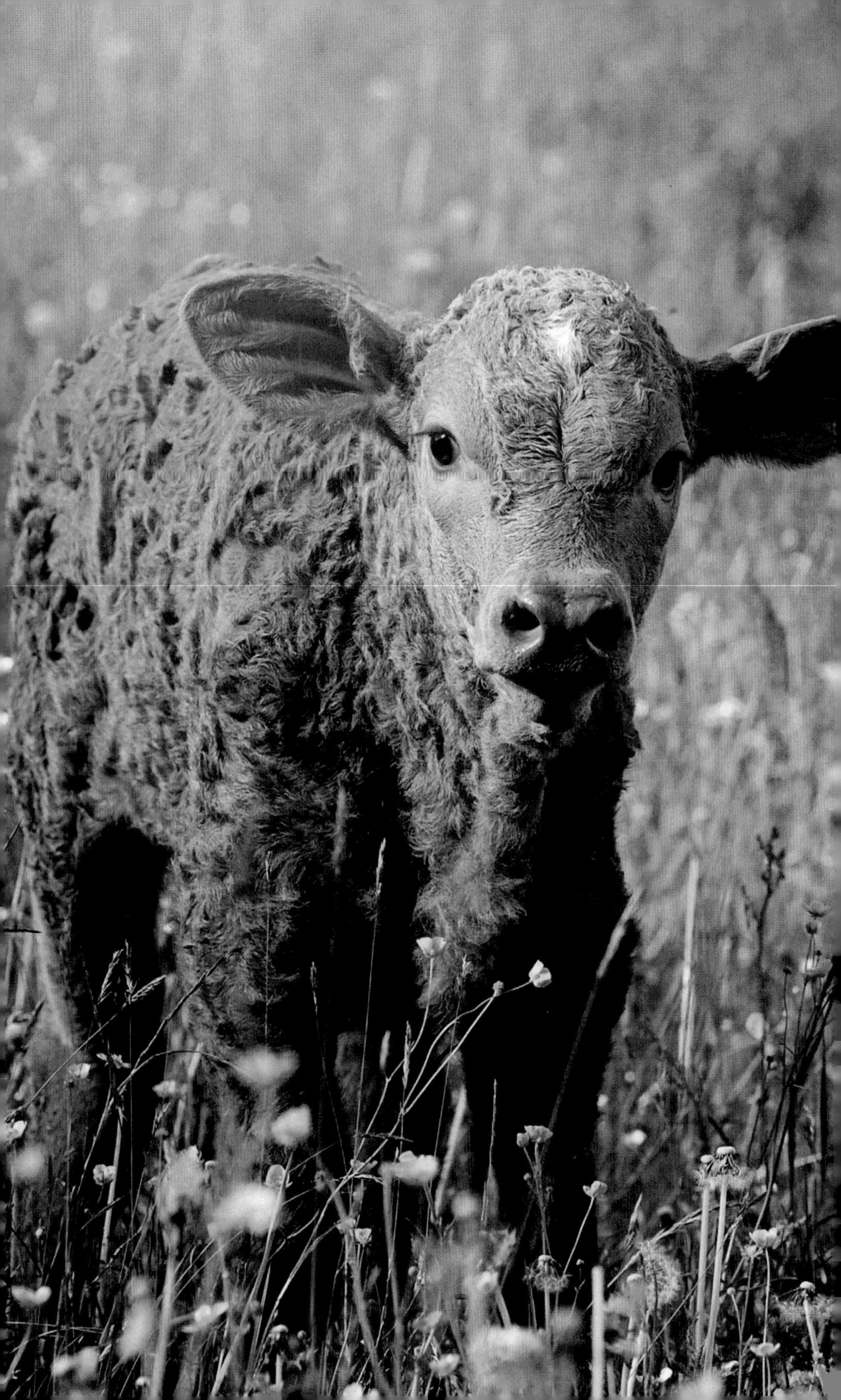

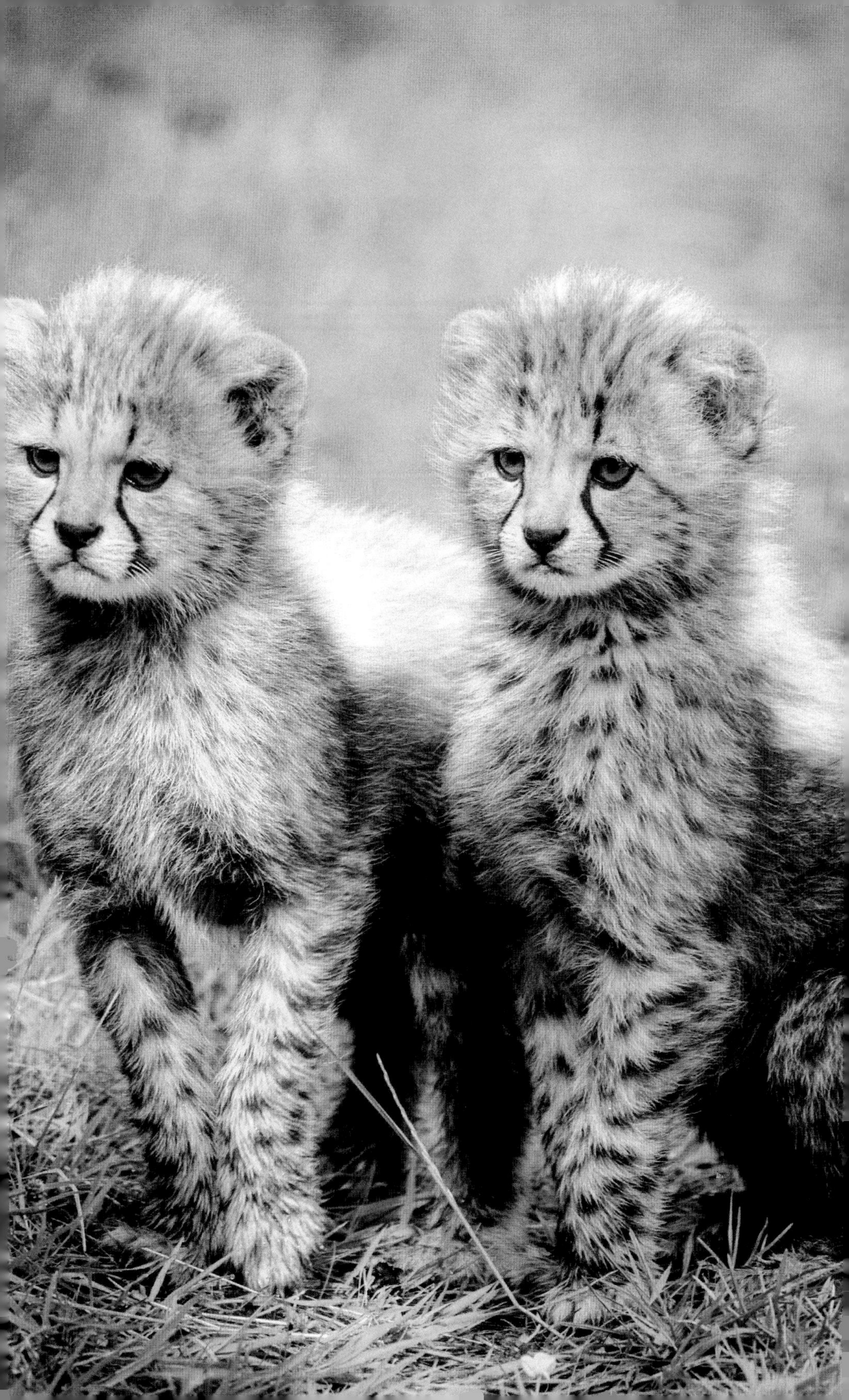

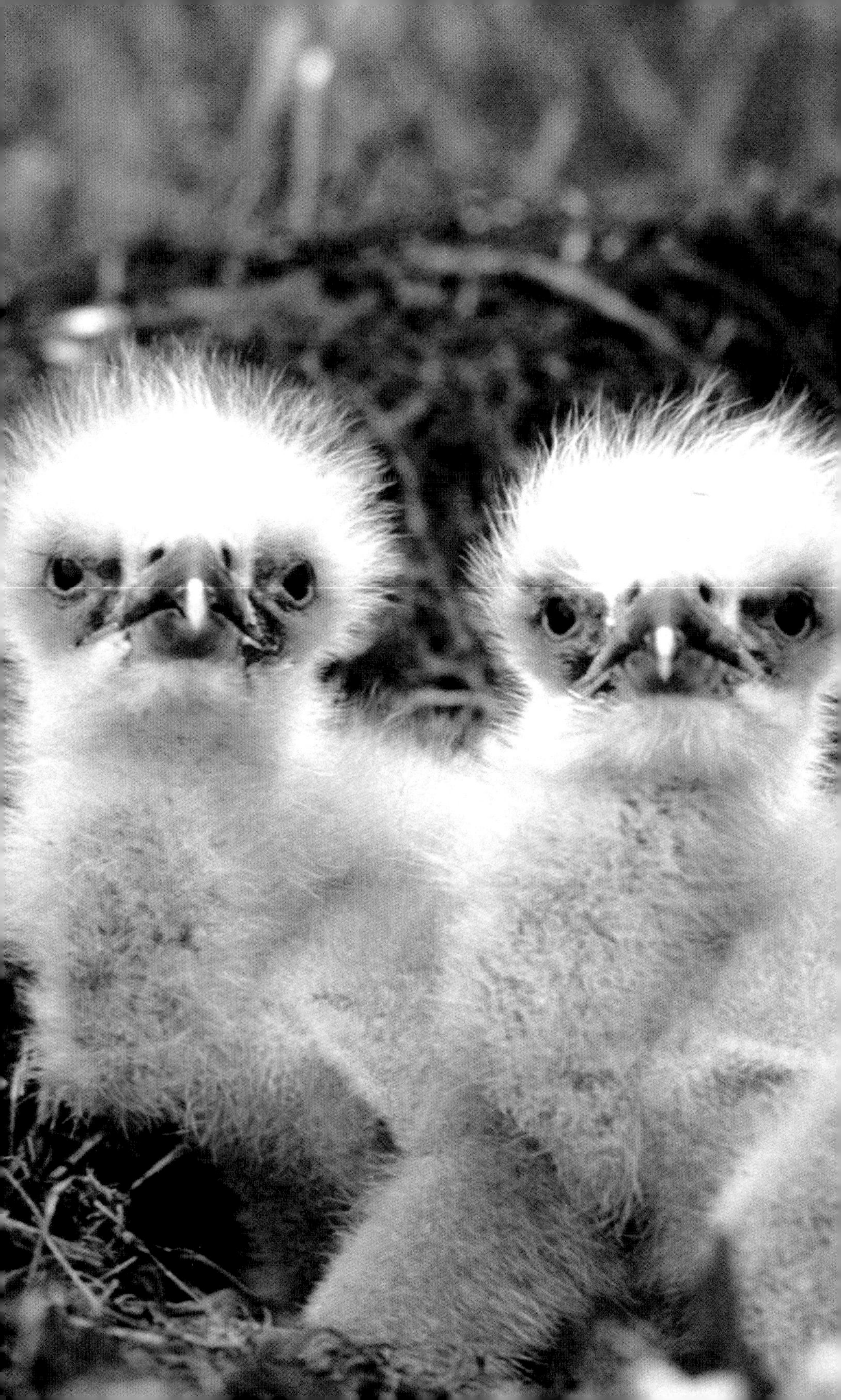

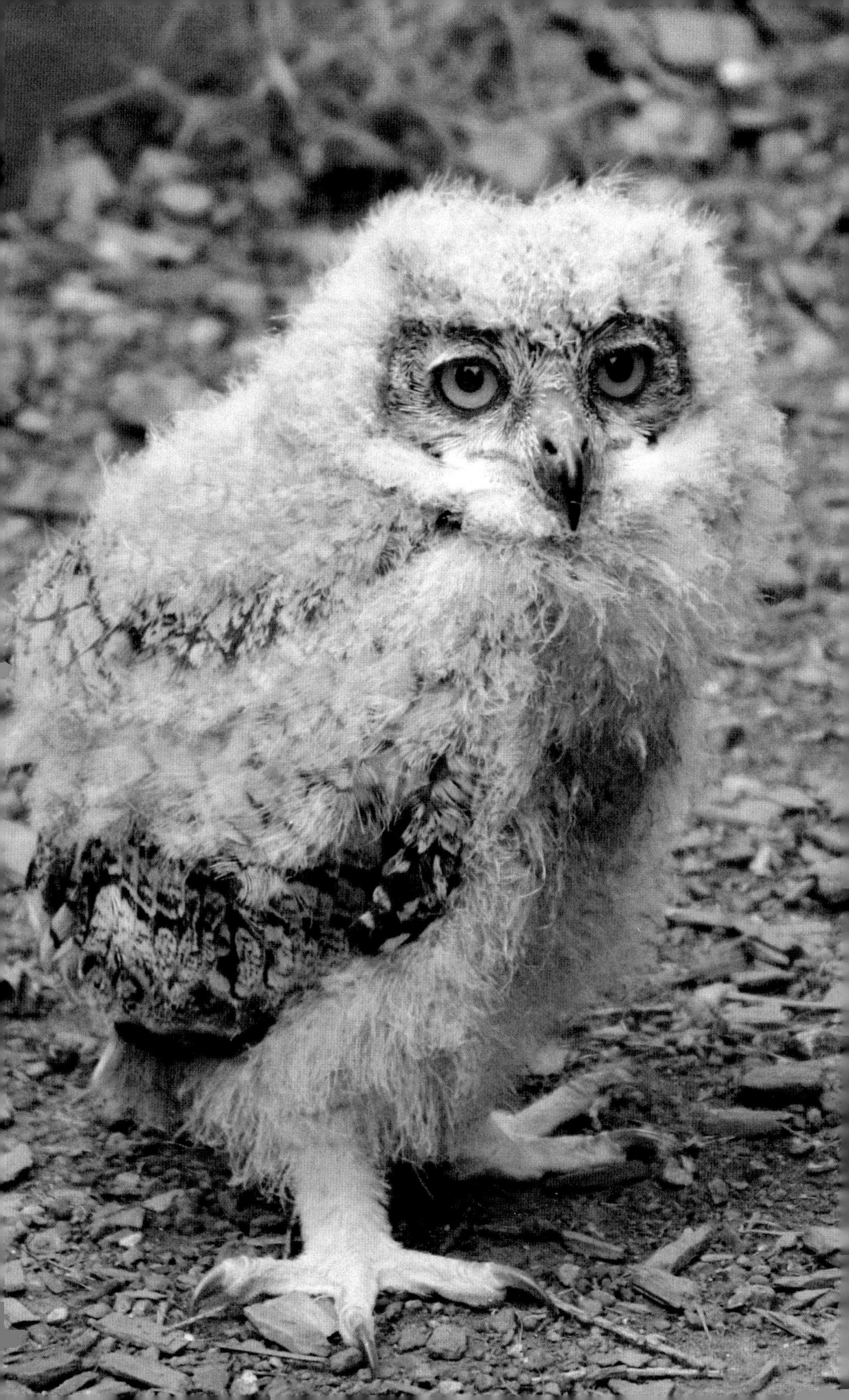

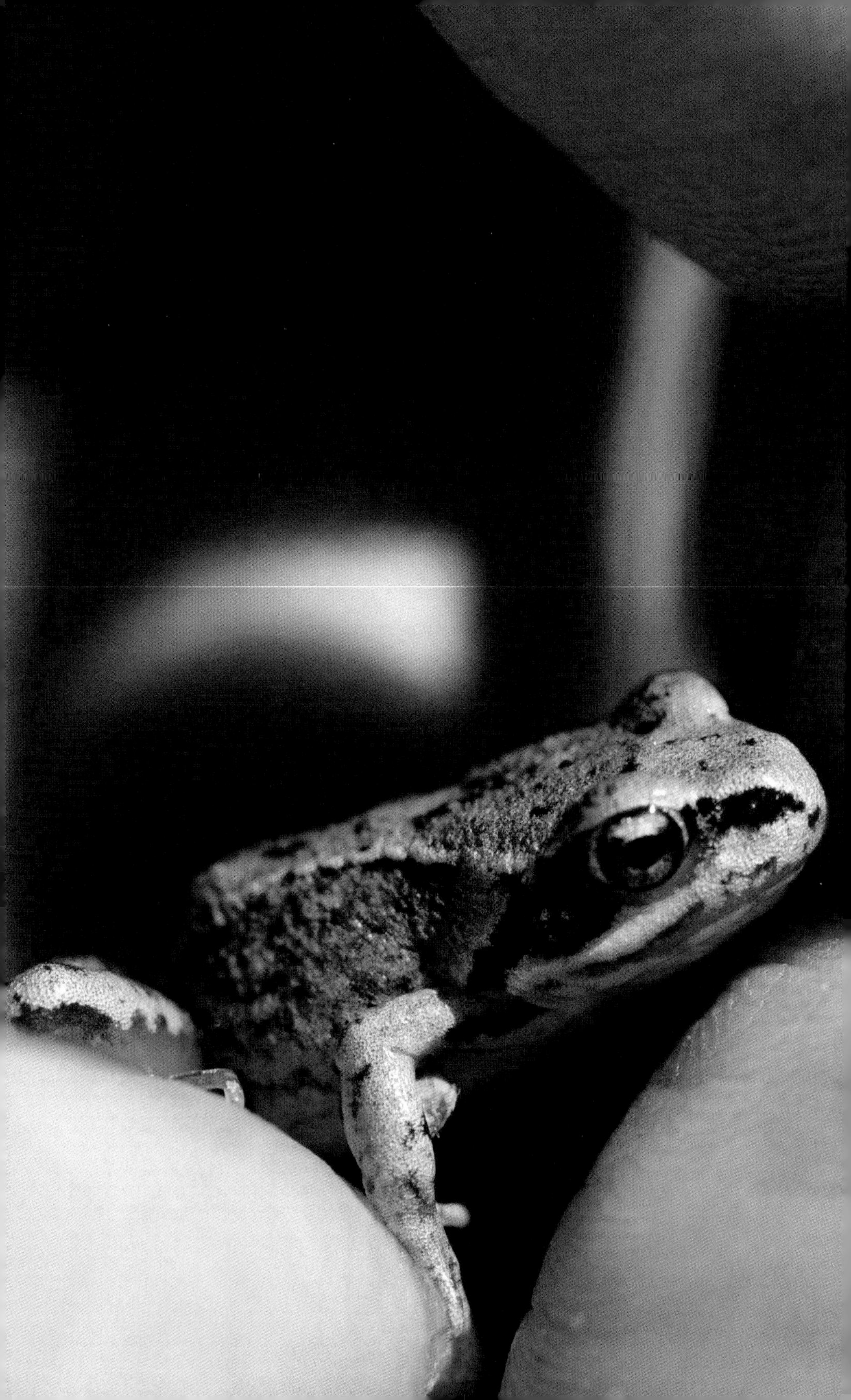

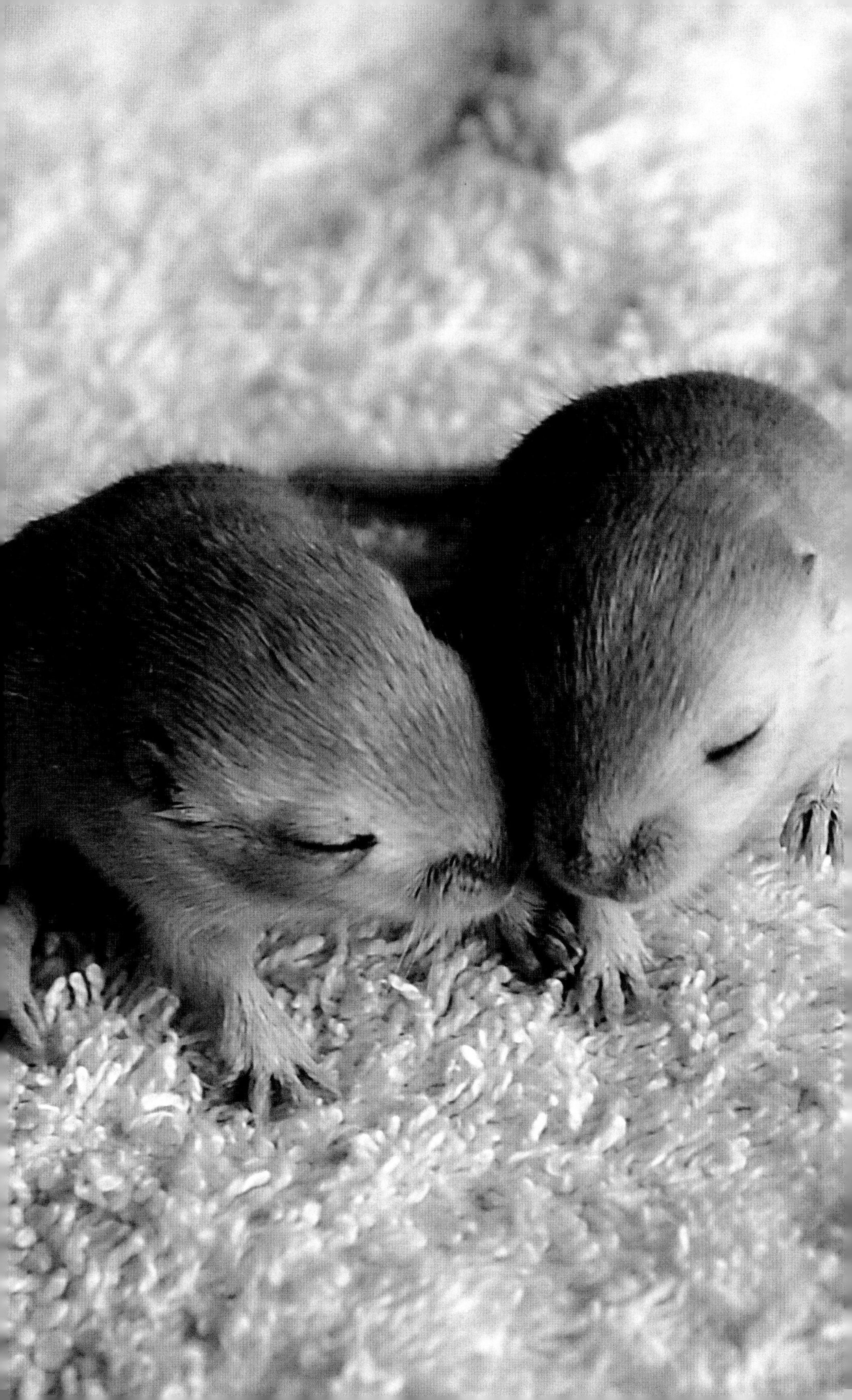

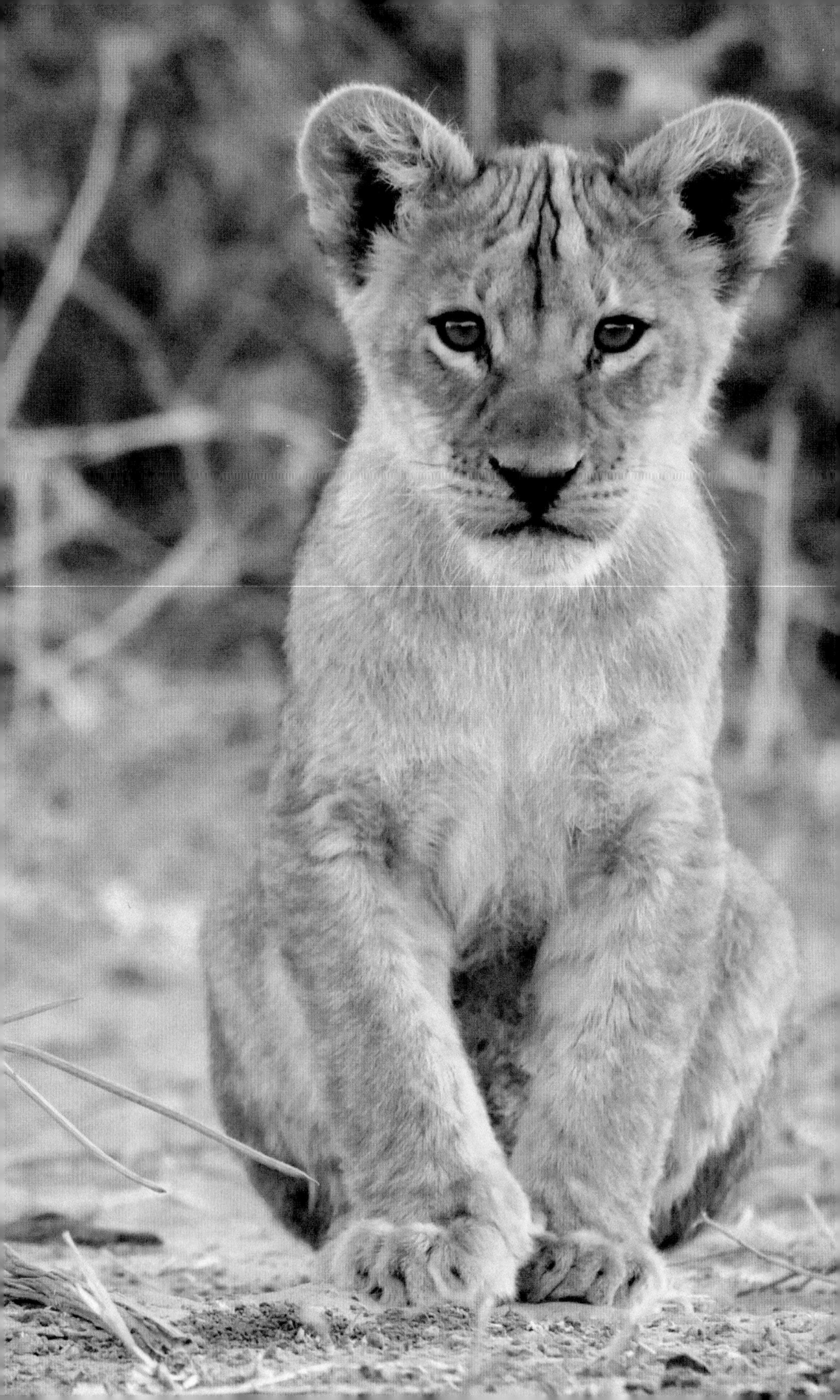

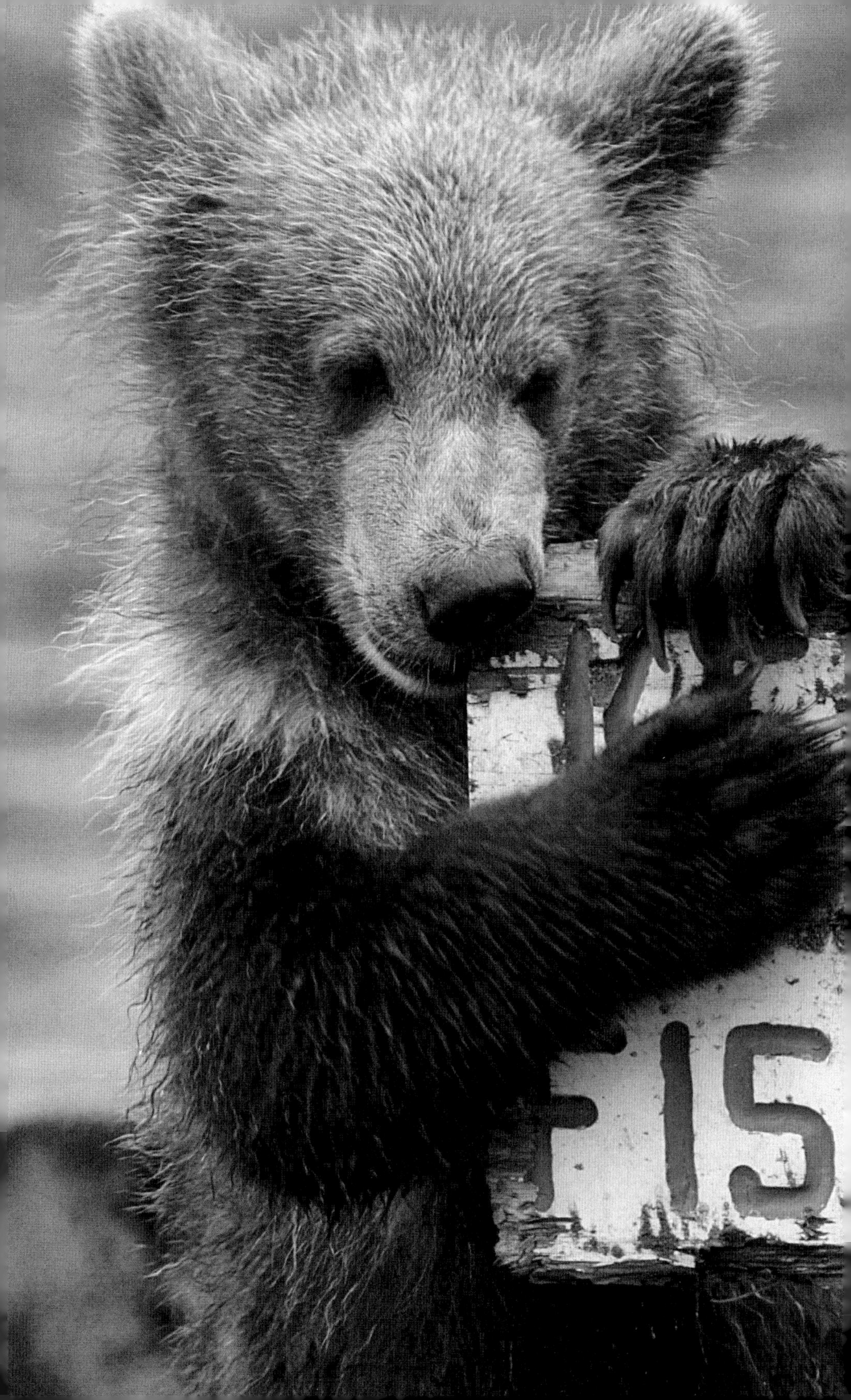
15

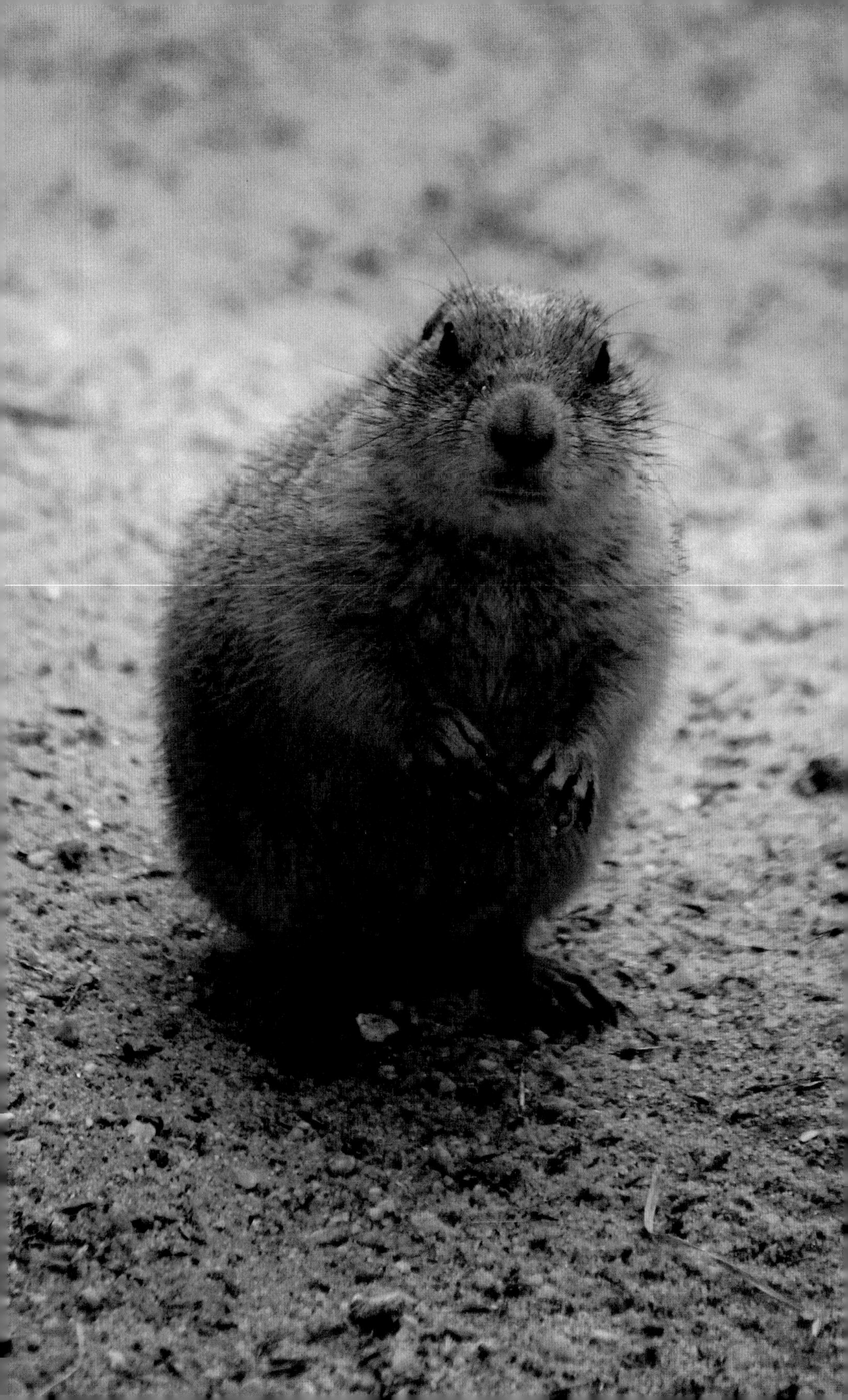

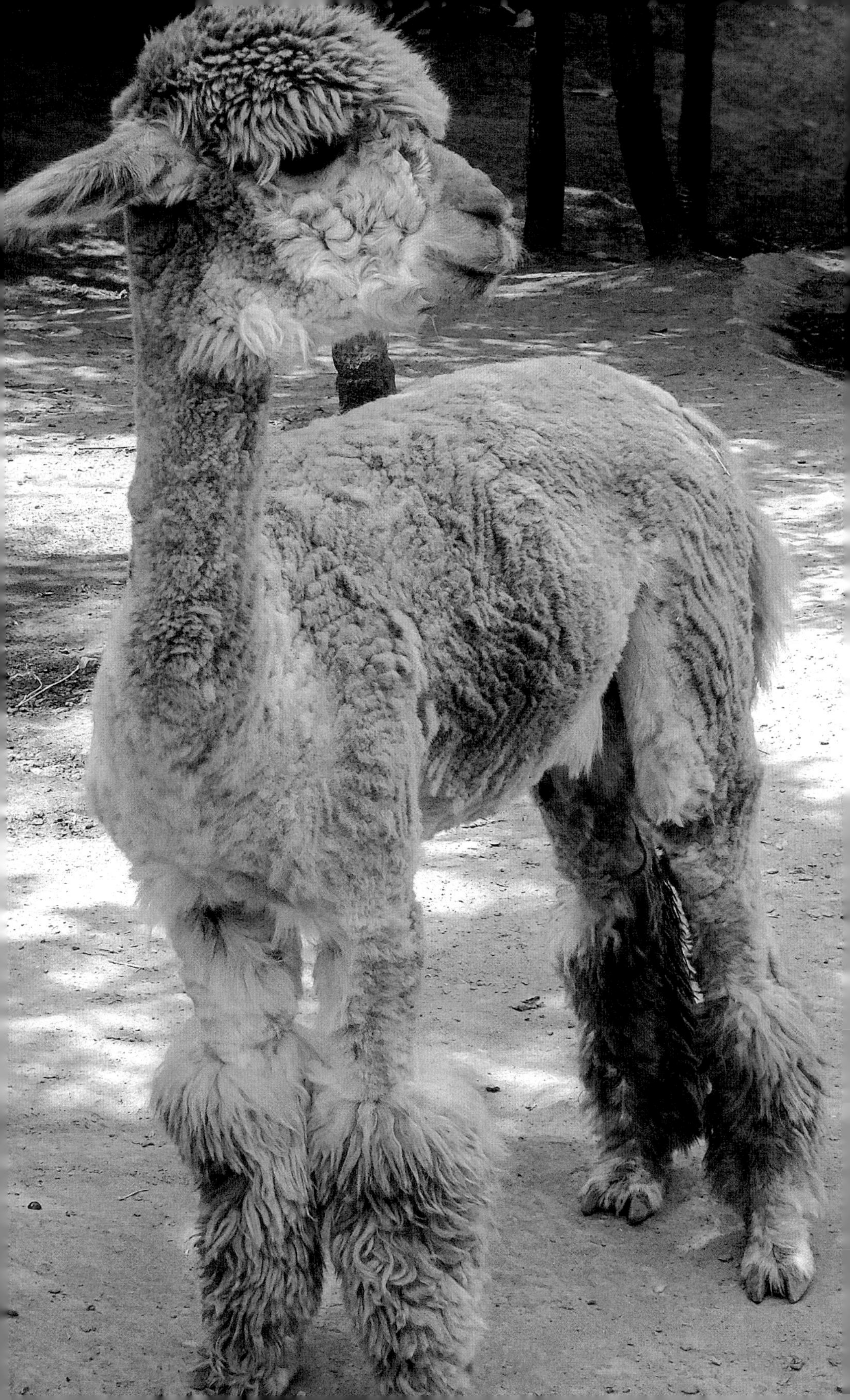

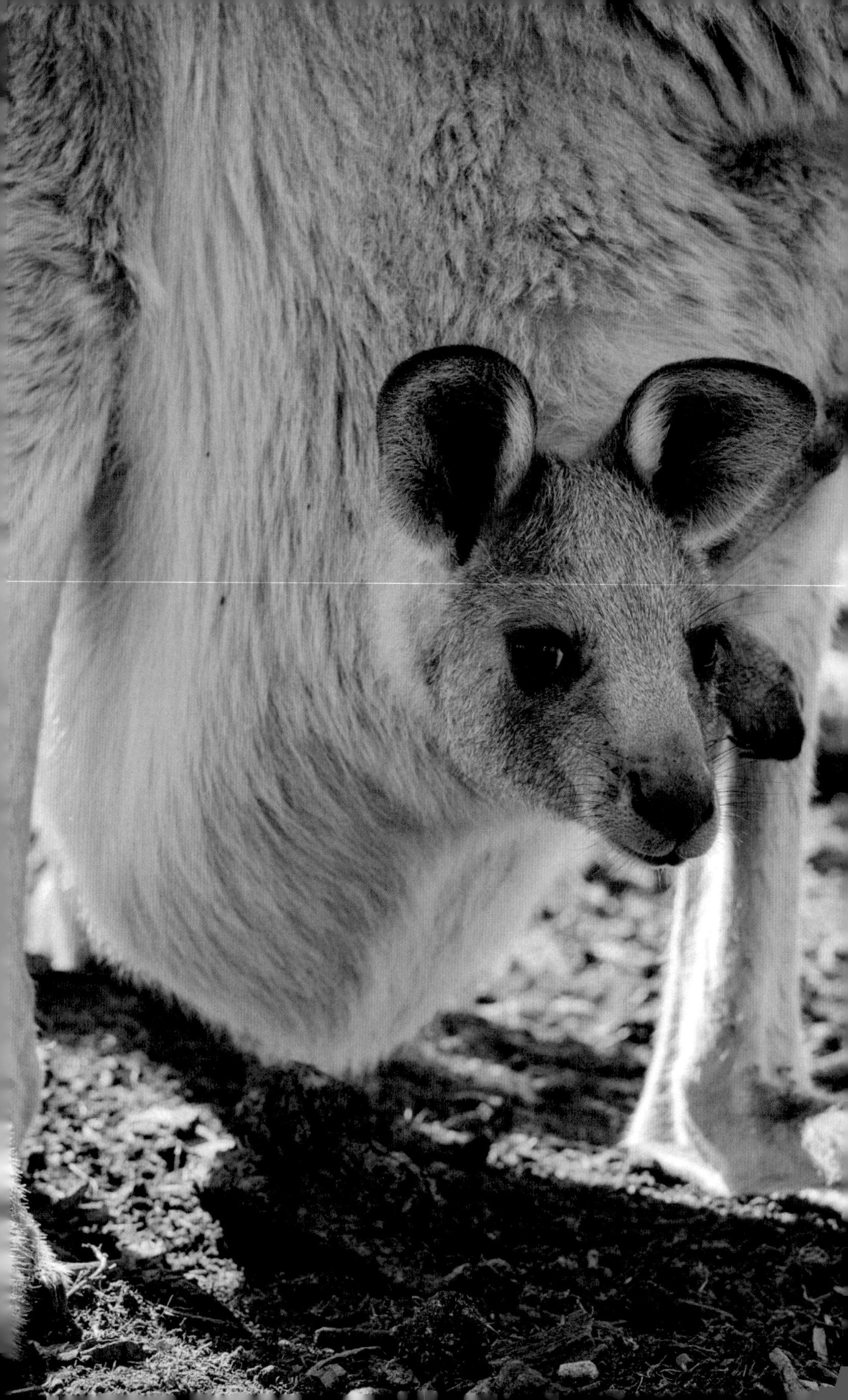

Made in the USA
Middletown, DE
11 June 2021

41868644R00024